businessbuddies

successful
performance
reviews

businessbuddies

successful
performance
reviews

Ken Lawson, M.A., Ed.M.

BARRON'S

First edition for the United States, its territories and dependencies, and Canada
published 2005 by Barron's Educational Series, Inc.

Conceived and created by
Axis Publishing Limited
8c Accommodation Road
London NW11 8ED
www.axispublishing.co.uk

Creative Director: Siân Keogh
Editorial Director: Anne Yelland
Design: Sean Keogh, Simon de Lotz
Managing Editor: Conor Kilgallon
Production: Jo Ryan, Cécile Lerbiere

NOTE: The opinions and advice expressed in this book are intended as a guide only. The publisher
and author accept no responsibility for any loss sustained as a result of using this book.

All inquiries should be addressed to:
Barron's Educational Series, Inc.
250 Wireless Boulevard
Hauppauge, New York 11788
www.barronseduc.com

Library of Congress Catalog Card No: 2004116959

ISBN-13: 978-0-7641-3243-8
ISBN-10: 0-7641-3243-1

Printed and bound in China
9 8 7 6 5 4 3 2 1

contents

Introduction

Whenever he wished to gauge his popularity, or public reaction to a new administrative policy, former New York City Mayor Ed Koch would pose a simple, pointed question to the media and citizens at large: "How'm I doing?" Koch, whose reputation was built on his outspoken leadership style, would then brace for the shower of bouquets and brickbats that inevitably followed. By the time all was said and done, he had garnered a wealth of useful information about his on-the-job performance. Koch's penchant for soliciting feedback served him well: He used it to resonate with New Yorkers throughout three colorful terms as Mayor.

Koch's famous catchphrase is the question that all employees wonder about: What is the quality of my job performance and what results will it bring? As a manager, it's your responsibility—and a significant part of your job—to deliver the answers to your reports, but likely not before you learn about your own performance from senior executives, who can keep you in your own job, move you up the ladder, or move you off it.

Performance reviews, or appraisals, are the occasions when employees and managers learn, sometimes with brutal frankness, just how well they are doing on the job.

Many employees and managers are not eager to participate in the appraisal process. Performance reviews are typically anticipated with a feeling of fear and dread because they are veiled in mystery and ambiguity. Employees wonder what nasty surprises and bad news may lie in store for them. Managers wonder how they can deliver criticism constructively and professionally, without sabotaging their leadership aura or compromising anyone's integrity.

Successful Performance Reviews lifts the veil on the mystery of the appraisal process. It provides a thorough explanation of the reasons for performance reviews, and their benefits to employees, managers, and organizations. Then, in clear, concise and easy-to-understand language, it shows exactly how the appraisal process proceeds; what needs to happen

Introduction continued

when a performance review is being delivered; how to prepare for this critical career event; and how to manage its aftermath.

In this easy-access guidebook, both managers and employees (and remember, most managers get appraised too!) will find dozens of detailed, step-by-step guidelines to the appraisal process and how it's carried out. You'll become familiar with the different kinds of performance reviews and the benefits and drawbacks of each. You'll learn how to manage the timelines and expectations that are attached to the appraisal process, and how to communicate clearly and effectively about them. And you'll learn how to create an action plan that addresses performance goals and promotes measurable career advancement.

By their very nature, the vast majority of performance reviews create an opportunity for career development and success that both managers and appraisees alike can leverage almost immediately. This is mostly what makes them so valuable. Throughout the pages that follow, your personal tutor prepares you for the appraisal process, coaches you in participating in it, and advises you on responding to it.

Successful Performance Reviews will help both managers and appraisees gain the insights to understand the review process thoroughly, and the resources to navigate it responsibly and effectively. It's an indispensable guidebook for any professional who needs to know "how am I doing"—and any manager who needs to provide the answers.

Ken Lawson, M.A., Ed.M.

Career management counselor and author

Instructor, School of Continuing and Professional Studies

New York University

purpose and principles

What is a performance review?

Performance review is the formal assessment by a manager (the "appraiser") of a subordinate's (or "appraisee's") work performance over an agreed period of time. Typically, this is carried out on an annual basis, but, as we shall see, assessment needs to be an ongoing process and shouldn't be limited to a once-a-year catch up.

If reviews happen more often, perhaps twice yearly, both the manager and subordinate will benefit. The manager will have a better chance of keeping productivity on track and the subordinate will have more up-to-date knowledge about his own performance, developmental needs, and the changing context of work. Usually, the assessment is formally codified on paper using a standard form, which is completed by the manager and countersigned by the subordinate. One form, with various adjustments depending on departmental needs, is often used company-wide, ensuring consistency across the workforce, whether the company is big or small. The form assesses the subordinate's performance on several levels. The assessment is discussed during a meeting (the performance review meeting or appraisal meeting) attended by the subordinate and the manager. In many companies, a follow-up meeting is arranged shortly after the performance review meeting to discuss reaction, commit to goals and objectives, give feedback on the performance review itself, and to "sign-off."

However, the performance review process is not just about filling in forms. In fact, in all well-run companies, the system is ongoing.

A MANAGER WILL:

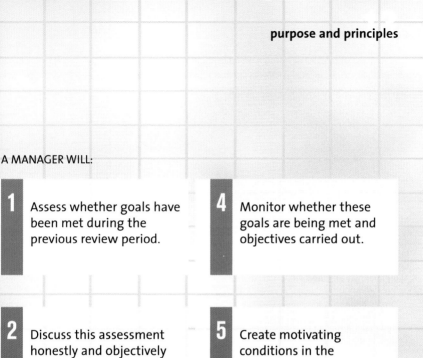

1 Assess whether goals have been met during the previous review period.

2 Discuss this assessment honestly and objectively in a review meeting with the appraisee.

3 Set new goals and objectives for the coming review period.

4 Monitor whether these goals are being met and objectives carried out.

5 Create motivating conditions in the appraisee's workplace.

6 Provide constructive feedback at each step.

Why use a performance review?

Performance review is an essential management tool on three different levels—individual, departmental, and organizational.

INDIVIDUAL

■ Feedback

All employees need and are curious to know how they are getting on. A formal process allows all aspects of an individual's performance to be assessed in a prearranged, objective way.

■ Improving performance

All employees need to know how well they are currently executing their responsibilities before they can be motivated to improve in weaker areas, or further build on good work. This also makes employees face up to any performance problem issues.

■ Determining pay raises

Pay raises are often determined by how positive a performance review an employee receives. Not all organizations choose to work this way, but generally, the better an employee is performing, the better his financial compensation. However, the compensation issue is also strongly related to the general business picture—sometimes pay raises are not possible even for the best performers if overall business conditions are gloomy.

■ **Renewal of the work contract**
Performance reviews often amount to renewal of the work contract. This occurs by revisiting the formal and informal commitment to the organization and its goals. A well-conducted review will leave the employee feeling as committed to the company as the day he began work. In this way, reviews effectively enhance employee motivation.

■ **Determine development needs**
Performance reviews enable managers to spot the development and training needs of their staff.

Why use a performance review? continued

DEPARTMENTAL

▨ Promotion
A performance review will show an employee's true value to an organization, allowing managers to promote subordinates, safe in the knowledge that their decisions are based on solid evidence.

▨ Redundancy
The flip side of the coin is that if a company needs to downsize, those with negative performance reviews can be identified as the first to go.

▨ Setting goals and objectives
This is a common and effective motivational tool. It clearly sets out measurable expectations of each employee. This is much more effective than the "just do your best" strategy.

ORGANIZATIONAL

▨ Talent spotting
All organizations need talented individuals. Performance reviews enable managers to spot where the talent is and also move talent around if it is unevenly distributed throughout various teams and departments.

▨ Retention
An effective appraisal system ensures that the most talented employees do not elect to leave the organization for another company.

Wider training needs
If all employees are showing a need for training in a specific area, then there may be a skills or knowledge gap throughout the organization. An organization-wide training need can then be identified.

Hiring staff
Managers can assess whether new staff are the talented individuals they seemed to be at interview, or whether they are merely filling the ranks. Recruitment success can therefore be evaluated.

Legalities
A demonstrable history of negative performance reviews can prove a valuable legal defense for any company being sued by former employees.

General organizational performance
The composite picture is that if all the points above are covered, overall organizational performance will improve—ultimately, this is the point of the whole performance review process.

Individual benefits

On an individual level, each employee will benefit from knowing exactly how he is performing at work, with regard to parts of the job that are going well, and parts where more attention is needed. These are the benefits each employee, regardless of status, will derive:

OBJECTIVITY
A good appraisal system objectively measures an individual's performance against predetermined standards, in a predetermined way, and honestly analyzes whether they have been met.

VALUABLE INFORMATION ON EXPECTATIONS, STANDARDS, AND RESOURCES
No one can meet expectations if he does not know what those expectations are. Individuals need explicit guidance on standards for output and quality, and the resources, feedback, development, and training that are available to help achieve those standards.

FEEDBACK
The fundamental point of appraisal is to answer the question, "How am I doing?" Performance reviews should provide this answer, based against objective, measurable criteria, the performance of others doing the same job, and in light of the values and culture of the company.

REALIZING EMPLOYEE POTENTIAL
Appraisal is the ideal time for an individual to bring up areas where he can make a significant contribution, and to explore career development as a whole. Bear in mind, though, that any aspirations must be realistic.

PAY RAISES

Pay and performance are increasingly linked. Although appraisal may not be the best time to talk about money (and many appraisal systems forbid this as a topic for discussion), an individual will at least be able to understand how the company's compensation policy works, and how any increase can be negotiated (see pp. 152–153).

TRAINING AND DEVELOPMENT

An individual will be as interested in training as their manager; training directly benefits both parties. Development on the job that leads to an increase in skills and experience is also critical.

AGREEING OBJECTIVES

This is different to being told what to do, since all individuals will expect at least some of their thoughts and views to be taken into consideration when planning for the next appraisal period. Subjects may include performance and quality, systems and processes, and personal development.

IMPROVING THE JOB

Suggestions from an individual on how efficiency, quality, and output can be increased can lead to their job improving. This will increase job satisfaction, which will in turn decrease staff turnover.

Managerial benefits

On a departmental level, the benefits of an effective performance review system are also invaluable. Broadly, performance review is designed to enable managers to get the best from their staff.

THESE ARE THE BENEFITS DEPARTMENT MANAGERS WILL BE LOOKING FOR:

1

SPOTTING THE HIGH PERFORMERS
All managers need to pinpoint who their most effective staff are. Conversely, they also need to know who their underachievers are. In short, they need to know the makeup of their department.

2

KNOWING WHO TO PROMOTE
Performance reviews will quickly reveal who is suitable for promotion. Again, if a company downsizes, performance reviews will also show who will be shown the door first.

3

KNOWING WHO TO COMPENSATE
Irrespective of promotion, companies often link good performance to pay raises. Performance reviews show who should receive any raises and can help gauge how much.

4 TEAM DEVELOPMENT
Performance reviews will highlight any shortcomings in
teamwork, and will pinpoint the natural leaders.

5 TRAINING AND DEVELOPMENT
Appraisal will highlight every employee's strengths and
weaknesses. Appropriate training and development programs
can then be created effectively.

6 MANAGER-EMPLOYEE COMMUNICATION
The value of a two-way feedback system cannot be
overestimated. No manager has all the answers and no
employee can work alone. Also, any grievances can be aired and
resolved. Effective communication, which starts with appraisal,
solves these problems.

7 GOALS AND OBJECTIVES
How can employees maximize their productivity if they do not
know what they are expected to achieve? Appraisal enables
managers to set targets.

Organizational benefits

While they have many advantages for employees at all levels of the organization, the ultimate main aim of performance reviews is to benefit the company implementing them. These are the overall benefits all companies will be looking for:

1 INCREASED PRODUCTIVITY
This is achieved by increasing the effectiveness of each individual employee. Remember that everyone in the company is an employee, even the CEO, and everyone is appraised by someone, even if the eventual appraiser turns out to be the shareholders or bank manager.

2 WIDER GOALS AND VISIONS
Performance reviews can help employees see the bigger picture and understand the changing nature of business environments and the position of their particular company within it.

3 ATTRACTING THE RIGHT APPLICANTS
In addition to retaining staff, companies that develop a reputation for developing and training their staff attract a higher caliber of applicant than those companies that don't.

4 LOWER STAFF TURNOVER
When management take a sincere and active role in assessing, listening to, and motivating staff, employees feel valued and are less inclined to seek work elsewhere. Retaining staff is important since the best performers need to be groomed for promotion; retention reduces the huge cost (and risk) of appointing new employees to replace the ones who have left.

5 PROTECTION FROM LAWSUITS
If performance reviews are carried out honestly, objectively, and professionally, companies that fire underperforming staff have a clear paper trail that can be invaluable in justifying their decision to a court.

What are you appraising?

You are appraising performance standards, and nothing else. It is essential that you do not stray beyond this basic concept. Standards can often include not just quantifiable issues, but behaviors, attitudes, and workplace style.

To assess performance standards fairly, your review system must be:

OBJECTIVE

Standards must be the same for all and understood by all, and not include any subjective opinions or feelings. This means assessing performance targets and deciding on a factual level what is and isn't an acceptable performance standard. Objectivity is a key area for conducting a fair assessment of an employee's work and is based on how observable that employee's performance is. Objectivity means avoiding making decisions that are based on:

- Popularity
- Favoritism
- Seniority
- Circumstance
- Luck
- Differences of opinion with management

MEASURABLE

In addition to being objective, you should assess an employee's performance on measurable criteria. The most obvious way of doing this is to observe quantifiable or "countable" performance. Examples include:

- Number of units produced
- Sales revenues reached
- Number of returns due to quality issues
- Budgets met
- Deadlines and timekeeping
- Time saved, time gained
- Number of new customers won

However, measurable does not necessarily mean quantifiable. There will usually be several aspects of performance that require a judgment to be made, and it is possible to be objective when making these judgments. Examples include:

- Employee's overall effectiveness
- Employee's creativity and contribution to ideas
- Contribution to team goals
- Employee's contribution to client satisfaction
- Attitude to work
- Initiative
- Employee's internal effectiveness—their "fit" with peers and other colleagues

Who carries out the review?

Performance review is collated from one or more of five main sources. Multiple-source appraisals are increasingly popular and are often called 360-degree appraisals.

THESE ARE THE SOURCES:

MANAGERS

These are the people most likely to carry out a review, since managers have direct experience of their subordinates' work, and will have been involved in setting subordinates' goals and objectives in the first place. Sometimes, a "grandfather" is involved. This is the manager's supervisor. Although he will not be directly familiar with the subordinates' work, this role can be useful since it reduces the likelihood of bias, and may allow the appraisee to see the bigger picture.

THE SUBORDINATE

All subordinates must review their own performance and be in a position to discuss their performance objectively in the performance review meeting; otherwise, no meaningful discussion can take place between a manager and a subordinate. This is not as hard as it sounds if tackled with maturity and honesty, and within set guidelines.

PEERS AND TEAM MEMBERS

When a company is not based on rigid hierarchical structures, and when there is no direct competition for promotions, valuable information can be obtained from fellow employees. Peers and team members can be empowered through this process to contribute to the development of the employee. To ensure that no employee should be made to feel that they are snitching, the process should be completely transparent, but confidential.

UPWARD APPRAISAL

Some feedback to the manager from those he has just appraised is essential in determining how successfully the appraisal was conducted. It also provides a valuable insight into management and leadership styles (see pp. 64–65).

CLIENTS AND CUSTOMERS

"Customers" is a catch-all term, now used to describe anyone who receives an employee's services, such as people inside the organization, perhaps in another department, as well as the obvious clients and customers outside the company who buy products or services (see pp. 92–93).

Different types of review

There are two basic types of appraisal, the casual, conversational type and the formal, form-based type.

THE CASUAL APPROACH

Use the casual approach if your company is small, or has just started out in business. Take out a blank sheet of paper and start making some notes, but don't suddenly spring a formal written document on your employee.

THINGS TO DO:

1 DO PREPARE
Just because this is a conversational style appraisal does not mean you can simply make it up as you go along.

2 MAKE ENOUGH TIME FOR A RELAXED MEETING
Casual does not mean rushed or getting interrupted by other work pressures such as phone calls.

3 BE SINCERE, OPEN, AND ENCOURAGING
Conversational does not mean you can be flippant, sarcastic, or patronizing in the way you speak.

4 INFORM THE EMPLOYEE OF YOUR INTENT FOR THE MEETING, AND THE PREPARATION HE MUST DO BEFORE THE MEETING
Casual does not mean you can avoid planning the meeting. Provide the employee with specific suggestions on what to look at and how to prepare.

5 PUT THE MAIN POINTS FROM THE MEETING DOWN IN WRITING
Get the employee to sign it or acknowledge it by return, or in the follow-up meeting, if one if scheduled. This way, you have a written document to work from—you will not remember all the points of a conversation in six months' time.

6 LISTEN TO WHAT THE EMPLOYEE IS SAYING
Many employees may be defensive at first. You must give them a sense that they are being heard. Do not let your attention wander or assume that because the style is conversational you can just dismiss some points or edit them out.

Different types of review continued

THE FORMAL APPROACH

The formal approach usually means filling in a standardized form, often produced and distributed by Human Resources (HR). These forms are common in large companies and are designed to ensure that fair comparisons can be made between all employees by asking them the same questions.

THINGS TO DO:

1

USE THE FORM
Fill it out completely and honestly, and do not attempt to create your own questions or ignore some questions as irrelevant.

2

FOLLOW ANY INSTRUCTIONS
The instructions will help you fill out the form properly. Often, these come with the appraisal form itself.

3

CONSIDER THE SELF-APPRAISAL
Some forms require an appraisee to appraise him- or herself in writing in advance of the performance review meeting. If so, consider the information you are given when completing the full appraisal form.

4 IF NECESSARY, ADD MORE TEXT
If the form is inadequate, or you believe that there are other
issues to be covered that are not mentioned on the form, attach
another sheet to add more text to the form.

5 USE THE RATING SYSTEM
If one is used, rate your employee objectively and on
measurable grounds only (see pp. 24–25 and 78–81).

6 TAKE TIME TO PREPARE
Formal or informal, both you and your subordinate must
prepare for the meeting, and know what is expected of you in
terms of its preparation and the points to be discussed there.
Also, different people react differently to the appraisal process,
so some will demand more time and effort.

What does effective performance reviewing look like?

The performance review meeting, or appraisal, typically takes place once a year. At its core is the idea that the previous year's work is discussed, assessed, and graded, and then a new set of goals and objectives are planned for the coming year.

These goals and objectives can be set in a separate follow-up meeting, carried out shortly after the performance review meeting, but can also be dealt with in one meeting.

Next, the subordinate needs to carry out these goals and objectives. However, how does any manager know if these goals are being met successfully? An annual meeting is not sufficient to keep track, although the formal meeting may only take place annually. For a performance review system to be truly effective, reviews should take place throughout the year. This allows the goals and objectives to be met, constant monitoring and feedback to be gained, and since circumstances change during the year, adjustments can be made to accommodate these changes.

As the subordinate's goals and objectives are met, the manager conducts a performance assessment, evaluating how well the employee is doing, and gives him the appropriate rating (see pp. 78–81). This assessment is discussed in the next performance review meeting and the process begins again.

1 PERFORMANCE REVIEW MEETING
Discussing last year's performance.

2 SETTING GOALS AND OBJECTIVES
Setting targets for the coming year, sometimes in the same
meeting, sometimes in a follow-up meeting.

3 COMMUNICATING PERFORMANCE
Learning and practicing communication skills needed for
the meeting.

4 ASSESSING PERFORMANCE
Evaluating if goals are being met, filling in the appraisal form,
and setting a rating.

5 MEETING THE GOALS AND OBJECTIVES
The employee carries out the goals and objectives.

purpose and principles

Legal requirements

There is no legal requirement for a firm to have a performance review system in place.

Appraisals are instigated solely by a company for the purposes of improving staff effectiveness and efficiency, and ultimately to develop a competitive advantage.

However, any review system, once up and running, must follow the rules of employment law. This is because an appraisal is considered to be an employment test, similar in nature to interviewing, hiring, promoting, and firing staff. Principally, the issue not to fall foul of is discrimination, and several laws expressly forbid discrimination at work on the basis of any of the following:

■ Race
■ Color
■ Ethnicity
■ Cultural affiliation
■ Nationality
■ Religion
■ Gender
■ Marital status
■ Pregnancy
■ Sexual preference
■ Age
■ Physical disability

This is codified in the Fair Labor Standards Act, Americans with Disabilities Act, Age Discrimination in Employment Act, and the Civil Rights Act.

Problems usually arise when a member of staff who has been performing poorly is dismissed. If previous appraisals have not been carried out accurately and objectively, and the member of staff has received acceptable ratings because, for example, he is well-liked or has been in the job for a long time, then he will argue that there was no reason to be dismissed. He may claim he has been discriminated against, based on the preceding list.

This is a very good reason to carry out appraisals honestly and objectively. Poor performers are always then rated poorly and, when dismissed, will find it very difficult to argue that they were dismissed for any other reason.

Actions taken against companies are typically brought by the Equal Employment Opportunity Commission (EEOC), who will require that the company justify its actions. A personnel record full of accurate performance reviews showing poor performance is valuable documentary proof for any company defending itself against such a suit. Good management practice may also stop a lawsuit from ever arising.

1 Make sure assessments are based on measurable criteria.

2 Make sure assessments are based on objective criteria.

3 Make sure assessments are based on workplace-related behaviors, not personality.

4 Keep the appraisal system simple (to minimize the chance of mistakes being made).

5 Be aware of all the legislation, old and upcoming, and monitor for discrimination.

6 Train appraisers (and appraisees) in effective appraisals. Develop a transparent appeals system.

ACCEPTABLE "DISCRIMINATION"

This is not to say that those employees who are performing well shouldn't be recognized for their performance. This recognition constitutes acceptable "discrimination" against those with poor performance records. There is nothing in law that says that companies cannot discriminate between employees on the basis of performance. But bear in mind that performance alone is the sole legitimate basis for discrimination.

This "discrimination" may seem to cause undesirable discord at work, but an important managerial task is to develop (and retain) the most capable and highest performing members of staff. These are the people vital to any organization's long-term success.

Once you have completed the performance review process, all managers should be able to point out what a poorly performing employee has to do to be treated more favorably, in line with the measurable and objective goals discussed in the review meeting (see pp. 24–25).

2

creating the process

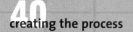

Who should design the system?

Who designs the performance review system is often down to the size of the company. Clearly, creating a system for a larger company that has lots of employees, lots of departments (perhaps on more than one site), and lots of managers all at various rungs on the career ladder will be a more involved and lengthier process than designing a system for an organization that has only a handful of employees.

Irrespective of the size of company, it is always wise to get input from a wide variety of sources. No one person will have all the answers or be able to cover all the bases.

CONSIDER GETTING INPUT FROM THESE PEOPLE:

1 HUMAN RESOURCES

HR is the obvious place to start. Often HR has the task of overseeing and administering performance reviews, as well as overall responsibility for any other systems that have an impact on employees. A well-established HR department will have experience of different appraisal systems and what has worked (or not) in the past. HR should be good at liaising with all departments and be well-versed in putting forward overall company vision.

2 CEO OR OTHER COMPANY "LEADER"
The top dog (who in a smaller organization may well have founded the company) sets the tone, style, and company vision. It is extremely important that these permeate into the appraisal system.

3 MANAGERS AND SUPERVISORS
Managers and supervisors are the people who really know their staff and everyday operations and problems. Also, middle-level managers are the ones who will be setting goals and objectives for staff and creating the conditions that motivate their employees and team members (see pp. 220–223).

4 CONSULTANTS

Advice from an external consultant is useful for companies unused to the appraisal process, or for those who have a process in place that is not achieving the expected results. A consultant is also useful if managers are relatively new, or the company has no experienced HR department to guide implementation, or the company needs help formulating performance measurement criteria.

5 COMMITTEE

A committee is a good way of involving all the key players at the same time. In addition to including the CEO, HR, and key managers, it is important to involve some staff. Only the staff know the day-to-day tasks and the problems that have an impact on those tasks. It will make them feel included and therefore valued, which can increase chances of staff retention. It also keeps issues real and opens lines of communication. For this reason, you also invite a representative from any trade union within your organization.

6 COLLEAGUES AT RIVAL FIRMS
There's nothing wrong with asking well-placed sources how the competition gets the appraisal process done. If you approach colleagues at rival firms with respect, most will feel flattered that you are requesting their advice—and may be more than happy to share it. But it's important to respect the privacy of colleagues at competitive firms and to honor their preference in providing you with guidelines or not. Do not expect, or seek, proprietary information.

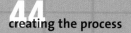

Is the system working?

The best way to determine whether a performance review system is working is to look at the figures. It is also possible to look at comments made on the appraisal forms themselves to see if the system is being administered properly.

1 WAS THE APPRAISAL PROCESS COMPLETED IN A TIMELY WAY?
Check to see whether all the forms and other follow-up processes were completed within the set timescale. If they were, this indicates a general enthusiasm for the process. If not, a degree of cynicism may be present, where managers are fitting in the demands of the appraisal as and when they have a chance.

2 CAN APPRAISAL RESULTS BE RELIED ON WHEN APPOINTING NEW STAFF OR DOWNSIZING?
If performance reviews are carried out reliably, their results can be very telling. Departments that are staffed with relative newcomers and that are receiving consistently poor ratings may have a problem with interviewing and appointing the wrong staff. In addition, ratings need to be accurate to allow a company to downsize effectively—they show who the poorest performers are, and these will be the first to be asked to leave.

3 HAVE THERE BEEN ANY COMPLAINTS?
A system that is working well will automatically attract fewer complaints from managers (and appeals from staff) than one that is not functioning properly. Bear in mind that there will always be some level of dissatisfaction. No process or system is ever perfect, and there will always be those who will quickly point this out to you.

4 IS THERE A CONSISTENT DISTRIBUTION OF RATINGS ACROSS DEPARTMENTS?
Notwithstanding general strengths and weaknesses of specific departments, a situation may arise where employee ratings in one department are much higher or lower than in others. This means that inconsistent standards are being applied, which must be addressed.

5 ARE YOUR STAFF IMPROVING?
Ultimately, this is the point of the appraisal system. Improving staff means a more competitive, productive, and profitable company. To see whether this is the case, and assuming all other conditions are equal, compare employee ratings for the current year with previous years' results. Appraisal should gradually create better performance.

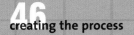

Improving the process

Even if your system if running smoothly and effectively, we live in a world where organizations and the business environment in which they function need to be flexible enough to change quickly if they are to maintain their competitive advantage. For this reason, performance review systems must change as well. An obsolete system cannot produce accurate results.

To improve whatever process you have in place, it is a good idea to do some checking and correcting. This process is called auditing, and it is best done once a year.

Spot-check the personnel files of a cross-section of employees. See whether appraisal forms exist and if have been completed fully. If not, this is an obvious place to start improvements.

TRY THE FOLLOWING:

Solicit feedback from HR on what problems or comments they are receiving. HR is often a good place to go when looking for general ideas for improvement.

Solicit feedback from your managers. Again, this is a very valuable place to go looking for feedback. Some pertinent questions to ask of your managers are:

- Have you been properly briefed on the appraisal system?

- Do you understand all elements of the paperwork?

- Are the forms easy to understand and use?

- Do the appraisal forms ask questions that are directly relevant to the appraisee?

- How useful is employee self-assessment (if used)?

- How easy is it to monitor whether goals and objectives are being met?

- How easy is it to monitor employees' personal development plans (PDPs)?

- How easy is it to follow-up on important points raised during the appraisal?

- What is your overall impression of the usefulness of the appraisal system?

- How have your staff reacted to regular appraisal?

- Has the system led to improvements in performance?

Solicit feedback from your employees. This can be done in a meeting in conjunction with some managers. Make sure you invite a good cross section to get a representative response.

Alternatively, if your company is large or you fear employees will not speak their minds in a meeting (this is often a well-founded fear), then consider circulating a survey to be completed anonymously. Ask whether the system is satisfactory, and if not, why not, and for any other comments. Bear in mind that an email is not an appropriate way of gathering comments—it is not anonymous.

Report on your findings—your employees will be expecting feedback from you if they are to believe that your request for information was genuine.

Designing a new process

Getting a new process off the ground is not an easy, quick task. You must make allowance for the fact that any performance review system is time consuming, never more so than when either getting one up and running from scratch or implementing a new one.

THESE ARE THE POINTS FOR YOU TO REMEMBER:

FIND OUT WHAT YOUR COMPANY MISSION STATEMENT, VALUES, AND VISION ARE
These are essential initial guidelines for deciding what is important to your company. Only the things that are important should be assessed by the performance review. To this end, you will have to ask senior management to get involved with making sure the organization's values are clear, and to back the process of implementing them in an appraisal process.

WHAT IS THE PURPOSE OF YOUR PERFORMANCE REVIEW SYSTEM?
What are you hoping the performance review system will give you? Do you want a method of finding out who to promote (or who to make redundant)? A way of deciding who gets pay raises and how much? A way of creating a system of feedback? A way of determining development or training needs? Whatever you decide, make sure that the emphasis is placed on the areas most important to your company.

KEEP IT SIMPLE

Make any appraisal instruments easy to follow, easy to use, and easy to implement. This is especially true in companies that have large numbers of employees. No one can sift through long and complex forms for hundreds of direct reports. See also the point on legalities (see pp. 34–37).

WHAT HAS WORKED BEFORE

Check what has been tried before. This means asking employees and managers who have been with the company for a long time what was a good idea, and what wasn't. This is to avoid repeating past mistakes.

DEFINE STANDARDS

Based on each employee's job description, the values and mission statement of your company, and the core and job-based competencies, determine what standards you want employees to demonstrate for each part of their job. As previously discussed, these standards can either be quantifiable in terms of being numerically provable, or relate to behaviors.

Designing a new process continued

ENSURE THE PLAN IS EFFECTIVELY COMMUNICATED

Everyone will want to know what your plans are for appraisal, and everyone will be cynical about appraisal if you do not tell them. This means that those whom you appoint to implement the system (often HR) need to be kept abreast of your developments regarding the form and how and when appraisal should be carried out. This principle of communication also applies to managers and employees. Send out requests for suggestions and comments from all parties.

ENSURE MANAGERS AND EMPLOYEES ARE TRAINED AND BRIEFED

Your managers must be fully informed of what is expected of them. This can only realistically be communicated properly in a training session that spells out the different parts of the whole appraisal system, and what needs to be done to fulfill each part of it successfully. This also applies to appraisees. Simply landing a form on someone's desk one day with the instruction to fill it out will not get a constructive dialog going. Appraisees need to be instructed on what they are supposed to do, why they are doing it, and what the benefits of appraisal are. And your enthusiasm for the process must shine through as well.

LEGALITIES

We have already seen how important it is to have an accurate record, provided by appraisal ratings, of employee performance when it comes to defending your company from lawsuits. Remember that your appraisal system must be able to withstand legal scrutiny.

MAKE SURE THAT:

1 The appraisee is clear what appraisal is.

2 Only job content and competencies (such as behaviors) are appraised, not personality.

3 Expectations and performance standards are clear from the outset.

4 The manager's completed form is discussed and signed by the appraisee.

5 Any right to appeal is made available to the appraisee and thoroughly followed up.

Getting your plan across

"Appraisals are a waste of time." "Appraisals are just another way for management to spy on us." "Appraisals are just another bit of company propaganda." "Appraisals mean jumping through a few hoops just to get them out of the way for another year."

These and more are, unfortunately, commonly held views on appraisal, and they come both from managers and their subordinates. The common denominator underlying the cynicism is a lack of trust in the value of the system itself, what it can deliver, and the intentions of those running it. In fact, lack of trust is the biggest hurdle to overcome in implementing a performance review system. Performance reviews can be quickly and easily undermined at all management levels, but particularly at grass roots level. If your rank and file staff don't believe in it, it will be always doomed to fail.

THESE ARE SOME BASIC GUIDELINES FOR SELLING THE IDEA OF PERFORMANCE REVIEWS TO ALL STAFF:

1 MAKE SURE THE SYSTEM INCLUDES EVERYONE
This means implementing performance reviews right across the board. In many instances, particularly in companies that employ lots of blue-collar workers, only white-collar workers get assessed. This smacks of elitism and creates an "us-and-them" mentality. This will not create the trust you are looking for between management and staff.

2 SEEK IDEAS FROM ALL STAFF
This means actively taking on board the concerns and
comments of staff at all levels (see pp. 40–43). The reverse
of this is what must be avoided. Top-down management
structures are very rigid and tend to believe that they do not
have to bother with the rank and file in a company. This is
unwise because it creates a culture of corporate snobbery in
senior management and low morale on the shop floor by
generating a feeling that whatever you say, your voice will
never be heard. Again no trust can be developed in this climate.

3 MAKE A POINT OF SHOWING STAFF THAT THEIR IDEAS
ARE BEING INCORPORATED
This is perhaps the most vital of all the selling tools available to
you. This doesn't mean that you have to use everything you're
being told, but show that some of it is useful to you—and you
can guarantee that some of it genuinely will be. Employees at
all levels will trust a system that they have helped create.

Training management

Clearly, if your management team doesn't understand (or worse, even want) a performance review system, the system will fail. This means that you need to train your managers in what to do, how to do it, what is expected of them, and why they are doing it. In short, the appraisal system must be delivered properly if it is to work.

Ideally, your appraisal system should be short, manageable, and easy to understand, but also ask the right questions in the right areas and so maintains its effectiveness.

THESE ARE THE ISSUES THAT YOUR TRAINING MUST ADDRESS:

THE ADMINISTRATIVE SIDE OF APPRAISAL This means:

1 Understanding how the form was designed.

2 Understanding the questions on the form.

3 Having the ability to fill in the form and use the rating system.

4 Understanding how to set up an appraisal meeting.

5 Understanding how to discuss the form with the appraisee.

6 Understanding how to ask for a self-assessment and the part it plays in the appraisal meeting.

THE PURPOSE OF APPRAISAL This means:

1 Understanding how appraisal fits into company vision and values.

2 Understanding why appraisal is necessary in increasing overall company performance.

3 Understanding all the benefits for the company.

4 Understanding all the benefits for the employee, in terms of satisfaction and motivation.

Training management continued

HOW TO GATHER AND USE INFORMATION This means:

1 Understanding the requirements of constructive feedback.

2 Understanding how to listen and build rapport.

3 Understanding job descriptions, key job responsibilities, and competencies, and where they fit in.

4 Concentrating on performance and behavior, not personality.

5 Being able to use the appraisal to make promotion and wage raise decisions.

6 Being able to see areas for improvement and knowing what to do about them.

7 Being able to see strengths and knowing how to improve on them.

8 Understanding how to facilitate the use of a development plan.

HOW TO MOTIVATE This means:

1 Understanding how to create motivating conditions at work.

2 Knowing how to create challenging, achievable, measurable goals.

3 Being able to build trust-based relationships with subordinates.

4 Knowing how to deal with persistent underachievers.

HOW TO LEARN

Learning is best achieved with role-play. Periodic training updates are also necessary to refresh managers' minds. Refresher courses are best run before the appraisal meetings start.

Inducting employees into the system

Employees need to be involved with, and fully understand, the appraisal system if it is not to become quickly mistrusted and derailed. This means that suddenly landing a form on someone's desk one morning with no warning is not the way to proceed.

Managers must formally explain to employees the following issues before they attempt to implement any part of the performance review system. Many of these issues mirror those that managers must get to grips with.

BY THE END OF THE PRESENTATION, EMPLOYEES MUST BE CLEAR ABOUT:

1 What appraisals are.

2 What the form is, how it is designed, what its significance is, and who fills out which bits.

3 The rating (or other scoring) system used for each section and any overall rating given at the end.

4 How the job description, key job responsibilities, and core and job-based competencies are used in appraisal.

5 How appraisals tie in with the mission statement, vision, or values of a company, and how they further those aims.

6 What role employees play at each stage of the appraisal process, what part managers play, and what responsibilities both parties have in making the system work.

7 How the system will benefit them in making them a more skilled, experienced, knowledgeable, and motivated member of staff than they would have been otherwise.

8 How they can prepare for the appraisal meeting, in terms of assessing their own performance and learning how to conduct themselves during the two-way conversation.

Since employees are not conducting the appraisal, coaching should not take long. Remember that, for the appraisal system to work, your staff must back it, trust it, and see results from it. Present proposed timetables, sample forms, and be prepared to answer any questions.

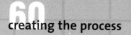

creating the process

Running orders and schedules

It is very helpful to write down, in order, the tasks that managers need to complete to fulfill all their obligations across the whole of the performance appraisal system. This is a sample list:

WEEKS 1–2
Work out who you are appraising.

Work out the number of people you are appraising.

These are:
■ Employees who work directly for you

■ Employees who used to work for you but have been recently promoted or transferred to other departments

Find out when the management training program is. Make sure you know when and where it is happening, who is organizing it, and make sure your name is on the list of attendees.

Find out when the employee induction program is. As before, make sure all those whom you will be appraising know when the induction session is. Make sure they know where to go and that all their names are enrolled. This is essential. Mistakes at this point will give an immediate bad impression to any employee who has been left out.

WEEKS 3–6

Attend the management training program. Receive the paperwork (the appraisal form, accompanying notes, self-assessments, templates for development plans, and any other specific notes issued by your company) from HR or headquarters. Make sure you have contact details for the department that is issuing them.

Start gathering all the information you need to prepare for the meeting.

Think about:
■ Job descriptions

■ Key job responsibilities

■ Competencies

■ Sources of information (peer review, customers and clients, 360-degree review)

Practice and read up on:
■ Rapport-building

■ How to give constructive feedback

■ Body language

■ Sample statements and appropriate language

■ How to deal with potentially difficult situations

Running orders and schedules continued

WEEKS 7–11
Give a self-assessment form to each appraisee, or ask for a list of accomplishments.

Have a premeeting discussion with each appraisee to draw up an agenda.

Start holding performance appraisal meetings.

Check that you have:
- Understood the need for objectivity

- Based your assessments on measurable criteria

- Filled in the form accurately

- Gathered evidence to back up all your performance ratings

- Completed all performance review meetings by end of Week 11

WEEKS 12–14
Submit all completed appraisal
forms to relevant supervisor/HR
as directed.

Analyze data from the forms and
follow procedure for linking
performance to pay raises.

Analyze data and link
performance rating to
suggestions for promotion.

Confirm pay raises and
promotions as appropriate.

WEEKS 15–18
Schedule goal-setting meetings
to set goals and objectives for
the coming year with all
appraisees (if not conducted in
the performance meeting).

Schedule informal performance
review meetings at specific
points throughout the year.

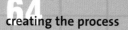

creating the process

Upward appraisal

Sophisticated organizations in which a considerable degree of trust has been built up between management and staff use a system of upward appraisal. As its name suggests, subordinates appraise their managers.

This appraisal takes place after the performance review meeting (and goal-setting meeting if separate) and is a written exercise completed anonymously. The paperwork is given to HR, who then give feedback to the manager so she can see how well she is performing, as perceived by her staff. This is also considered to part of 360-degree appraisal.

As with all appraisals, written forms are provided; they can take almost any form you care to think of. To be most effective though, they should be kept short and focus on key aspects of the manager's job.

SOME EXAMPLES OF RELEVANT QUESTIONS INCLUDE:

- How well has your manager demonstrated core organizational values?

- How clearly have goals and objectives been set?

- How has your manager facilitated your achievement of your PDP?

- How has your manager motivated you? Provide examples of challenges and recognition.

- How well has your manager supervised your performance in terms of providing constructive feedback?

- How well has your manager taken the initiative in arranging timely meetings?

- Identify areas of exceptional performance by the supervisor, with specific examples.

- Identify areas of performance by the supervisor that need improvement, with specific illustrative examples.

Alternatively, the employee may be asked:
- Your manager should be doing more... Why?

- Your manager should keep on doing... Why?

- Your manager should stop doing... Why?

In each case, a few brief examples are asked for. The important question of "why?" is also asked, which encourages the appraisee to think through the consequences of various managerial behaviors rather than just complain about something that irritates her.

Electronic appraisals

As more and more material is available online, written forms are becoming outdated in all walks of life, including performance reviews. Online, electronic performance review forms are becoming increasingly popular.

THESE ARE THE ADVANTAGES:

PAPERWORK IS REDUCED
The obvious advantage of working onscreen is that you don't end up with piles of forms to sift through. Nor do you end up with piles of last year's appraisal forms taking up valuable company space. Also, administrative costs are greatly reduced, from postage costs to HR man-hours used in organizing distribution.

PRINTING AND DISTRIBUTION COSTS ARE REDUCED
Forms cost money to print, and paper is expensive to buy and heavy, making it expensive to distribute. For large companies with thousands of employees worldwide, a significant saving can be made by avoiding the paper route.

MANAGERS CAN ANALYZE DATA MORE EASILY

If the information is already onscreen and can be easily downloaded into spreadsheets or other pieces of financial and management software, significant time and money savings can be made in extrapolating the most relevant and important information.

CHANGES CAN BE EASILY MADE

No review system can stand still for long. Onscreen performance reviews can, by their electronic nature, be changed quickly and easily as requirements demand.

MANAGERS HAVE AT-A-GLANCE REMINDERS

Managers with lots of staff can more easily track them when training or development requirement needs to be addressed, or when deadlines for certain goals or objectives are coming up. It also helps managers keep track of their own obligations. This is important. Managers who forget meetings or let some issue slide do so at the risk of creating cynicism about appraisal.

Electronic appraisals continued

POINTS TO BEAR IN MIND:

- Internet-based appraisal systems can be time consuming and expensive to set up.

- Once up and running, they require IT staff to manage and maintain them.

- Managers and employees may "hide" behind onscreen forms because it may be easier to do something online than conduct a controversial face-to-face meeting in person (or even on the phone).

- Confidential information can be hacked into by malicious outsiders, people within the company snooping for information, or disgruntled employees looking to erase negative information. The online site needs to be secure.

APPRAISAL SOFTWARE

Conducting appraisal electronically should not be confused with the variety of software programs that purport to give the right answers to any number of performance scenarios. These are to be used with caution.

Remember that:

- The performance review system requires integrity and trust to make it work well. Repeating stock phrases that are not your own automatically undermines this. No appraisee is going to have much time for you if she finds she is being appraised on the basis of what your software suggested you say.

■ Even if you are just looking for some hints or examples of what to say, you run the risk of quickly becoming dependent on the software for all your answers, to the extent that you end up saying the wrong thing altogether. No software is subtle enough to take into account how a meeting between manager and subordinate is progressing, or more general issues such as the core values of the company, both of which are some of the real determining factors in what you say.

■ Effective performance reviews are a management skill that you must commit to learning well, developing your own style along the way. Software can be viewed as a corner-cutting "cheat" that will not help you develop your management skills in the long term.

In cases where poor appraisal reviews lead to an employee being dismissed, no court is going to look favorably on your terminating someone's livelihood on the back of a stock set of phrases that were not your own and were applied inappropriately.

Continuous assessment

Once-a-year appraisal with perhaps two review meetings is a highly effective tool for assessing staff and formally getting feedback on a range of issues. The next step in taking performance review further is to provide managers with a platform for continually assessing staff. This is called performance management.

"Continuous" is a slightly misleading term, because it implies that everyone is assessed on a daily basis. For the purposes of performance management, "continuous" means three to four times a year.

DO YOU NEED ONE?
Performance management is demanding but done correctly with belief and enthusiasm is extremely effective. Because the process is year-round, its advantages are reinforced.

BENEFITS FOR THE ORGANIZATION

1 More productive staff

2 Engaged staff, leading to enthusiasm and staff retention

3 Open communication between managers and staff, leading to accountability and clear expectations

4 Better managers, experienced in management and goal-setting

BENEFITS FOR THE EMPLOYEE

1 More involvement with the company, leading to feeling valued

2 Regular opportunities to have good work recognized—this is a major motivator

3 Regular opportunities to have their input heard

4 Chance to build trust and loyalty

Can you handle it?
In essence, the system is very progressive and requires that company to have a certain type of management philosophy. First, the system requires constant two-way communication between staff and management.

Continuous assessment continued

Only companies that recognize the value of two-way communication should implement it.

Second, only companies that recognize the value of continuous development and learning, and regularly identify opportunities for their staff to learn and develop, are suitable candidates for performance management. This requires a particular organizational culture and philosophy, setting aside time and money for development both internally and externally, and not letting day-to-day issues have an adverse impact on this.

Small companies are obvious contenders for implementing systems like these because their logistical problems are much smaller than those of large companies, whose staff may be spread out over several sites.

Just like implementing appraisal systems, implementing performance management in large companies requires the full backing of senior management, who need to be prepared to make the time to monitor the whole system.

WHEN YOU SHOULDN'T USE CONTINUOUS ASSESSMENT

These are the types of conditions that indicate that your company is not yet ready for implementing a performance management program:

WHEN THE STANDARD APPRAISAL SYSTEM IS NOT TAKEN SERIOUSLY

It will be impossible to put a performance management program in place if your organization is not fully behind the more basic concept of performance review.

WHERE THERE IS A "NO-TIME" CULTURE

The "no-time" culture involves a heavy emphasis on tasks in hand, with little time for performance management techniques. Unless this culture can be changed (and change is likely to be gradual), then continuous assessment cannot be successfully implemented.

WHEN NO TWO-WAY COMMUNICATION EXISTS BETWEEN STAFF AND MANAGEMENT

Continuous assessment demands openness. If your company has a rigid top-down structure, performance management may not be suitable.

THERE IS A LACK OF TRUST BETWEEN STAFF AND MANAGEMENT

This is evidenced by high staff turnover and lack of morale. Continuous assessment demands openness and trust and will not work without it.

STAFF DO NOT WORK TOWARD CLEAR GOALS

You can assess performance accurately only if your staff know what their goals and objectives are, and this applies to performance reviews as much as continuous assessment.

TRAINING AND DEVELOPMENT ARE UNIMPORTANT

Because performance management emphasizes identifying areas for development, the system will not be suitable for companies that do not train staff.

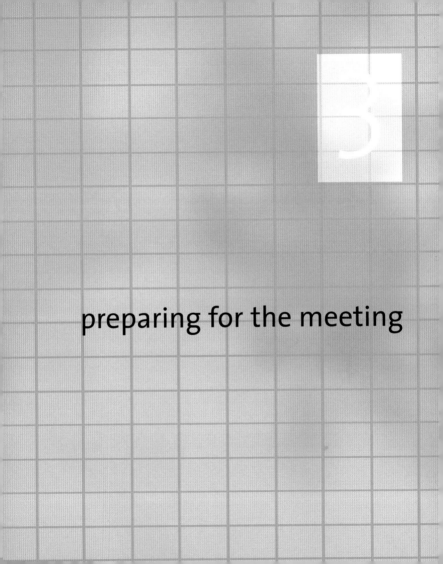

preparing for the meeting

What should a manager consider?

Preparing for the meeting requires a manager to assess the employee's performance over the past year (or period since last appraisal) and to learn about the communication skills that will be vital in conducting a two-way conversation. Many managers view the appraisal meeting as the most testing part of the whole performance review process.

IN ASSESSING AN EMPLOYEE'S PERFORMANCE, A MANAGER MUST CONSIDER:

1 The goals and objectives discussed and agreed at the last meeting.

2 The employee's job description, key job responsibilities, and competencies.

3 The employee's accomplishments.

These are often covered in a self-assessment form. If not, it is still best to list these on paper. Remember, these accomplishments must be based on measurable and objective criteria.

1 Fill in the appraisal form, as appropriate.

2 Review and discuss the completed appraisal form with the manager's own supervisor.

3 Think about any changes that need to be made to the original list of goals, objectives, and job description as laid down in the last meeting, in line with changing conditions.

4 Prepare for the face-to-face performance review meeting by deciding on language, style, and tone.

Measuring performance

So how should a manager measure just how successful an employee has been over the past year? Your assessment notes, as well as the self-assessment notes from your employee, will tell you whether or not goals and objectives have been met. But this is not a black-and-white matter. No one is entirely successful, nor a complete failure. There are degrees of performance that need to be measured accurately and then communicated to the employee.

THIS IS DONE IN THREE MAIN WAYS, USING:

1 A ratings system

3 A narrative system

2 A ranking system

A RATINGS SYSTEM

As its name suggests, this method involves using a ratings scale for each important part of the appraisee's job. Each part is then given a score, often on a scale, typically 1 to 5. This type of system is very common and appears on most performance review forms.

POOR

For example, let's take six important aspects of a customer care assistant's job:

- Speed of work 1 2 3 4 5
- Quality of work 1 2 3 4 5
- Communication skills 1 2 3 4 5
- Initiative skills 1 2 3 4 5
- Teamwork 1 2 3 4 5
- Attitude 1 2 3 4 5

Each of these can be given a scale of 1 to 5, with 5 being excellent, and 1 being poor. The manager simply rings the most appropriate score for that employee's performance. Very quickly, a clear picture of the assistant's performance of his key tasks can be built up.

Each score requires a definition. These are the typical definitions given to rating scores:

These are the characteristics of poor or unsatisfactory performance:

- Repeatedly makes the same, or very similar, mistakes

- Needs constant supervision

- Cannot follow a brief or other clear instruction

- Cannot spot own mistakes

- Has poor relations with colleagues and clients

- Has poor attendance or punctuality record

Measuring performance continued

MARGINAL

These are the characteristics of
marginal performance:

- Has difficulty completing
  a task

- Makes several errors

- Works slowly when compared
  to others in the same position

- Needs considerable supervision

- Misunderstands briefs or other
  instructions

- Is often unable to achieve
  quality standards

- Sometimes has poor relations
  with colleagues and clients

- Is sometimes late or absent
  from work

AVERAGE

These are the characteristics of
average or adequate performance:

- Works to agreed standards

- Is able to adapt to demands of
  new projects or clients

- Is able to comprehend and
  interpret briefs or instructions

- Has good relations with
  colleagues and clients

- Needs little supervision

- Makes some errors but is able
  to spot them

- Shows initiative

- Is not usually late or absent
  from work

GOOD

These are the characteristics of good or superior performance:

■ Produces work beyond that which was agreed

■ Works more quickly and accurately than those in the same position

■ Can work unsupervised for long periods

■ Popular with colleagues and clients

■ Can easily follow instructions and expand on them

■ Spots own errors and corrects them

■ Can cope with complex tasks

■ Makes suggestions for improvements

EXCELLENT

These are the characteristics of excellent or outstanding performance:

■ Consistently exceeds agreed goals and objectives

■ Can work quickly and to a consistently high standard

■ Can work unsupervised

■ Is expected to take the lead

■ Has valued opinions, which are constantly sought

■ Is a natural leader, encouraging those around him

Measuring performance continued

A RANKING SYSTEM

Although ratings create a clear picture of an individual employee's performance, rankings create a direct comparison between the performance of more than one worker in the same position. Rankings seek to show which employee is the most successful overall in key tasks. As an example, take three employees: Mr. Evans, Mr. Jones, and Mr. Smith. Each one is ranked according to his success in three areas: Quality of Work, Speed of Work, and Teamwork. A rankings table would look something like this, with 1 being the top rank and 3 the lowest:

Mr. Jones would receive the best overall review, since he has the lowest total. However, mention would need to be made of where performance was good and where it was poor, in order to highlight areas for encouragement and areas for improvement.

	EVANS	JONES	SMITH
QUALITY	1	2	3
SPEED	3	2	1
TEAMWORK	3	1	2
TOTAL	7	5	6

NARRATIVE

Narratives are commonly part of many performance reviews. These are an essay-style descriptive piece of prose detailing the state of play as regards an individual's performance. They are used because they allow for a departure from rigid, formatted parts of the evaluation form, and work best when they are considered as a supplement to rankings or ratings.

They are not often given much weight on an appraisal form because they require writing skills a manager may not have or need to have and also invite a subjective approach to appraisal because no predetermined criteria are given. An employee may have worked well and exceeded his objectives in one area, but if this is overlooked, or thought not important, then no credit will be given.

Also, because no mark, rank, or score can be deduced, it can be difficult to assess accurately the success or otherwise of an employee's performance. This can be a particular problem if pay raises are linked to performance.

An example might be: "Mr. Jones has been working under my direct report for six months now. During this time he has gone to great lengths to make sure that he understands accountancy procedures in this department, has shown initiative in suggesting new ways of working, and has developed strong relationships with key members of the team.

"He has shown himself to be cooperative and motivated; his attendance record is very good, and I would consider him ready for promotion in six to nine months time."

Avoiding bias and other pitfalls

These are the main problems that managers face in honestly appraising the performance of their subordinates. These should all be recognized and taken into account when preparing for the meeting.

■ **Popularity**
It is very difficult for both managers and subordinates to be frank. After all, they need to work together day after day, and a poor performance review can have a detrimental effect on work relations.

■ **Vested interests**
A poor performance review will have an impact on the manager as well as the subordinate. It will make the manager's own performance questionable, too.

■ **Honesty**
It can be difficult to be honest about your own performance. In our own minds, we are all good at our jobs. Why should an appraisee potentially harm himself by admitting to his boss that he is anything other than a great performer?

■ **Other's opinions**
The "grandfather" (who is your own boss and acts as an overseer and adviser), customers, and peers (see pp. 26–27) may have an incomplete idea of how well an employee is performing. Even if they do have a firm idea, they may not take into account how the employee is doing it.

▇▇

▦ Bias
Preconceived ideas about age, gender, race, and background can find their way into the appraisal process and color the final performance review results.

▦ Politics
The performance review system should not be used as a weapon to punish a subordinate. Conversely, misusing promotions to promote an employee "out of the way" is unacceptable as is creating competition between members—who will get the pay raise or the promotion?

▦ Ratings systems
Many appraisal forms require managers to give a mark, often on a scale from 1 to 5. Many managers seek to avoid confrontation by giving an average mark, neither too high, nor too low (see pp. 78–81).

Competencies

Another way to measure performance is to compare it to a set of predetermined skills, attributes, and behaviors, often called competencies, or behavioral criteria. Usually, top management decide what these competencies are. There is usually some standardization, but there is often no single absolute definition of what they are.

SUCH COMPETENCIES FALL BROADLY INTO TWO CATEGORIES:

1

CORE COMPETENCIES
These are the competencies that all members or staff must show, irrespective of seniority. "Sales awareness" and "acting with honesty" might be core competencies.

2

JOB COMPETENCIES
These are the competencies that apply to jobs that share the same characteristics. Creative employees in advertising companies might have to demonstrate "presentational" competencies. These might be preparing materials that show how an idea might be visualized, producing pilot commercials, and speaking in front of a group. Project managers might have to show "planning and organizational" competencies. These might include interviewing and hiring relevant staff, controlling budgets, scheduling, and managing logistics.

Competencies are useful because they eliminate subjectivity by providing a list of benchmarks to measure performance against.

Using competencies as a performance measurement tool requires managers to select what they regard as the most important competencies for that job and to assess the degree of success the employee has had in fulfilling that competency.

Managers must be careful, though, to ensure that the competencies are as specific to the job as possible. Comparing performance to vague or irrelevant competencies will cause a distorted appraisal result.

Problems measuring performance

We have already touched on some of the problems associated with the appraisals as a whole. More specifically, these are the problems associated with accurately measuring performance.

1

THE HALO AND HORN EFFECT
If an employee is given a high rating in one area (say, speed of work), this can have an distorting impact on the next area (say, teamwork), by creating a rating that is higher than it should be. This is called the halo effect, where the second rating basks in the "haloed" glow of the first. Conversely, the horn effect occurs where a low mark in one area spills over into the next area, creating an artificially low rating. Both effects must be guarded against by assessing each area completely independently and objectively.

2

CENTRALIZING RESULTS
We have already seen that giving a poor performance rating may upset manager-subordinate relations. Many managers give a middle rating of "3" or "average" or "satisfactory" to avoid confrontation. Of course, this may not be a true reflection of the real state of affairs. As we have seen on pp. 34–37, such lack of candor can lead to potential legal issues.

To avoid this, some companies use a scale of 1 to 6, where no middle or "average" number exists.

3 DIFFERING STANDARDS BETWEEN BOSSES

No two bosses are the same, and both will demand different standards. Thus two employees in the same positions but with different bosses may get different appraisal results, despite performing as successfully as each other.

This is where a "grandfather" (the manager's own supervisor) is useful, since he can act as moderating influence. Consistency can also be achieved by using the same form and guidelines company-wide, and effectively training managers in appraisal techniques.

Problems measuring performance continued

4 BIAS

Managers have to be on guard not to let their personal opinion about an employee distort their real assessment of that individual's performance. Well-liked individuals are likely to receive an overinflated performance result and vice versa. Refer to pp. 24–25 on objectivity to help overcome this.

This bias becomes more serious if it develops into stereotyping or prejudice, where it is assumed that success or otherwise is determined by some assumed (and erroneous) predisposition. Such issues often amount to discrimination and can be the basis for legal action (see pp. 34–37).

5 FAILURE TO ASSESS THE WHOLE YEAR

It is essential that the whole year is assessed when arriving at conclusions about work performance. This means not just discussing recent work performance but starting at the beginning of the year and working your way through performance methodically. This is harder to do than it sounds. In a fast-paced business environment, it can be difficult to remember issues that arose months ago and that now seem like history.

6 DEFINING MOMENTS

Managers should also not just look at a few great (or terrible) moments, or at single "defining" moments during the year. This is a big challenge for managers. Defining moments, especially negative ones, really stand out in managers' memories. Appraisees often complain that such moments take up too much time in the review meeting. All of these may mask other important factors in deciding on your final assessment.

Gathering input

An employee's performance cannot be fully assessed unless all available information is gathered. Even though managers may have the clearest picture, they may not be the only ones to have direct contact with the employee. We have seen how 360-degree appraisals work (see pp. 26–27), but this is an advanced technique to be used with care.

1 Peer-to-peer reviews require a great deal of trust. Do not add this component to an appraisal system until the department is ready for it.

2 Reviews on an individual's performance from co-workers must be anonymous. Also, the number of questions on the review form must be kept to a minimum, be kept simple, and be kept very specific to that individual's job.

3 When asking a client or customer about a subordinate's work performance, do so with the knowledge of the employee. The best time to let the employee know you will be asking customers for feedback is when you are setting goals and objectives, right at the start of the appraisal period. This gets the idea out in the open right from the word go.

4 How do you know when the circumstances are right to implement peer-to-peer and 360-degree appraisals?

■ There is open communication between staff

■ Employees have been working together for some time and know each other well

■ There is mutual respect between staff and management

■ Staff morale is high

■ Teamwork is good

■ Disputes between staff or between staff and management are rare and are handled professionally when they do crop up

■ Managers have been fully trained in how to handle these types of appraisal techniques

Looking at job descriptions

A job description, task list, or something by a similar name is another important piece of documentation that will help you to assess how well an employee has performed. If a proper job description is in place, then, in a similar way to competencies, a list of predetermined criteria can be used to assess performance.

In many instances, however, job descriptions are not accurate. This is because either the job description was not written accurately in the first place or the appraisee's job has changed, making the existing description obsolete—it may state key tasks that no longer apply to the employee's work. Most descriptions become obsolete very quickly, as business needs shift and as the employee shapes his job around individual performance. Job descriptions are best used as a point of reference for recalling why the job was designed. This means that a job description must have flexibility built into it as it needs to change as the appraisee's job changes. Nevertheless, the description will help all managers see what an employee's real job is, by allowing him to compare the duties listed on the description to "real" day-to-day activities.

If the job description needs updating, prepare to discuss which areas need attention and what they need to be changed to in the performance review meeting.

A PROPER JOB DESCRIPTION MUST SHOW:

1 Full job title, with department name, and any code or numbering system attached to that job (for example, a payroll number).

2 Status of the job, whether full-time, part-time, or temporary.

3 Federal Labor Standards Act status, either "exempt" or "nonexempt." Salaried staff are exempt; those on hourly rates are nonexempt.

4 The manager the employee reports to.

5 An overview of the job's purpose. This may take the form of a brief summary.

6 The specific, fundamental tasks, duties, and responsibilities that the employee must demonstrate to fulfill his role. These are formally termed "essential functions."

7 Other peripheral duties and responsibilities.

8 List of key skills and abilities the employee must demonstrate to complete the job successfully.

9 The list of physical attributes the employee must have to complete the job successfully. This becomes very important when dealing with employees with disabilities, who are protected by law under the Americans with Disabilities Act 1990.

10 The date on which the job description became active. This is important because the duties of a job may change over time, and the job description may have to be revised at regular intervals to keep it up to date.

An accurate job description, just like an accurate and objective appraisal form, is a useful tool for a company to defend itself against a suit for wrongful dismissal. If the dismissed employee did not fulfill the duties clearly stated on the job description, then he will have difficulty bringing the suit.

Learning how to give feedback

Performance reviews are really all about feedback. The manager honestly answers the employee's question "How am I doing?" However, the way in which you give feedback is as critical as the content of what you say, regardless of whether it is positive or negative. All of these rules equally apply to the appraisee.

SO, EFFECTIVE FEEDBACK IS:

1 CONSTRUCTIVE

Constructive feedback is a powerful motivational tool, intended to lead to improvement. It encourages good performers to perform even better, and stops feedback on poor performance from sounding like destructive criticism. The ultimate aim of the performance review process is to benefit the company, and well-delivered constructive feedback will further this goal.

2 RELATES EXCLUSIVELY TO WORK

What occurs outside work and has no bearing on performance at work, or any effect on the good name of your company, is not a subject for discussion in a performance review meeting. At all times choose your words with care. The ultimate aim of appraisal is to boost company performance. Poorly chosen words will quickly demotivate staff and ultimately decrease company performance.

3 ASSESSES PERFORMANCE, NOT PERSONALITY

The sole issue that managers must concern themselves with is appraising performance. Your views on the traits of your subordinate are irrelevant, unless he is having an adverse impact on team effectiveness.

4 SPECIFIC

Feedback should relate to the agreed competencies, job descriptions, and goals set in the last meeting. Specific examples must relate directly to the responsibilities and goals attached to the employee's job.

5 ACCOUNTS FOR PERCEPTUAL DIFFERENCES

Take into account that the way you see an employee's performance may be very different from how that employee sees his own performance. It is easy to draw conclusions from quantifiable results, but other less quantifiable issues may be harder to assess in "absolute" terms.

6 OBJECTIVE

Make sure that your assessment and measurement is objective and nonemotional. Avoid subjective opinions, and particularly avoid flippant, catch-all phrases such as "You always…" or "Everyone knows…"

Learning about communication

Learning how to say things is as essential as deciding what to say. Managers should also learn about the ways in which they will communicate, specifically during the appraisal meeting. The following points should be practiced extensively before the meeting. As with the previous section, these tips are equally as applicable to the appraisee as to the manager. Trying to make it up during the meeting won't work.

CONFIDENCE

As the manager, it is up to you to take the lead. You must come across as confident that your assessment of your employee is accurate. If a manager hesitates, repeats himself, stumbles over his words, becomes long-winded, is difficult to follow, contradicts himself, deviates from the point, and uses vague language full of words such as "maybe," "perhaps," and "possibly" he will come across as being unsure of what he is saying. This may lead to the employee questioning the performance review. So speak clearly, stick to the point, use definite terms, and practice being able to say what needs to be said without talking around the point.

STATEMENT OF PURPOSE

No appraisal conversation should start without a clear breakdown, given by the manager, of the format for the meeting at the beginning of the meeting. This will enable the employee to give clear, well-formulated answers, and will keep the meeting to the point and to schedule. So outline all the main points that will be discussed in the meeting. For example, say: "This morning we will be discussing three main issues. We will review your performance for the past year, then move on to future goals and objectives, before finishing with a development plan for you for the coming year. We will follow the structure of the appraisal form throughout."

RAPPORT

It will help greatly if the manager can establish a rapport with the employee. The conversation will flow much better, more will be discussed (and to a greater depth), and the meeting will be conducted in a more relaxed atmosphere.

To establish rapport, practice the following before the meeting:

■ Making eye contact (not staring)

■ Speaking in calm, even tone

■ Relaxing your face, so it doesn't appear twitchy or nervous

■ Listening without interrupting

■ Sitting in neutral, open position, comfortably upright, feet flat on the floor, hands in your lap or on the desk

■ Practice your opening lines. These can be ice-breakers, such as: "Did you see the game over the weekend?" or "Did your visit to the in-laws go well?" Beware, though, of giving the impression that this will be a casual conversation, so don't dwell on your first few words.

TWO-WAY CONVERSATION

Remember that you are not a judge or inquisitor. It is very important that your communication is a two-way process. The employee will be an adult who will have also prepared for the appraisal meeting and should have plenty to say about his own performance. Prepare for the meeting by establishing a series of questions that will draw the appraisee into the discussion. Typically, these are open-ended questions that provoke more than just a "Yes" or a "No" response. They often start with the words "How," "What," and "When." Avoid "Why," though, as this can sound like you are demanding an explanation and will put the appraisee on the defensive. We will come across these again on pp. 134–137.

Also, avoid interrupting the employee as he speaks. This always sounds dismissive and will irritate the person trying to get his point across. Listen attentively, and let the appraisee finish before replying. This active listening technique will be discussed again on pp. 134–137.

preparing for the meeting

Asking for lists of accomplishments

Managers must also ask the appraisee to prepare for the meeting. As we have noted earlier, this request for preparation often involves filling out an official self-assessment form. If your company uses self-assessment, make sure that you issue the appraisee with the form in plenty of time, at least 10 days in advance of the meeting.

LIST OF ACCOMPLISHMENTS

If no self-assessment form is used, request that the appraisee draw up a list of accomplishments. This is more informal than a self-assessment, and the appraisee can complete this exercise on a simple piece of paper or in an informal email. Note that the list is one of accomplishments only. Provide some guidelines for how you want the information to be structured. Do you want broader information, such as projects that have been successfully completed? Or would precise initiatives that have saved time and money be more relevant? The manager is not looking for a list of failures or mishaps.

This is a very valuable motivational tool. The appraisee will immediately recognize that they are being asked to list all the positive things that they have done over the year, and nobody minds being open about his or her successes. It also puts the manager and whole appraisal process in a good light. Often appraisees regard the appraisal process as an excuse for management to chastise them for their faults and failings. Asking for accomplishments makes appraisees think that management are actually trying to help people build on their previous successes.

TWO-WAY HELP

A list of accomplishments actually helps both the manager and the appraisee. For the manager, the list (or self-assessment) will remind him of all the things that Mr. Jones has done over the year. This serves as valuable prompt of what to take into account when filling in the appraisal form. Nothing is more embarrassing (and damaging) than omitting from the discussion (and the form) a project that Mr. Jones completed successfully at the beginning of the year, which the manager has since forgotten about.

Also, the list provides managers with a valuable insight into how appraisees view themselves and their performance, and the issues that the appraisee will expect to be discussed in the meeting. If the appraisee writes only a short list, or one that is only full of minor successes, alarm bells should start ringing in the manager's head. For the appraisee, such lists bring the year into focus; you are asking him to think clearly about his successes. Ask the appraisee to deliver the list (or self-assessment) to you some days before the meeting (you agree on a timetable in advance) to allow you to review it before filling in the form.

POOR PERFORMERS

Asking for a list of accomplishments is not appropriate when dealing with poor performers. Such lists will only distort the main message of the appraisal: the appraisee must improve. This becomes contradictory if the manager is holding a list of accomplishments in one hand, while spelling out how and why performance must improve.

preparing for the meeting

Dealing with the form

Appraisal forms come in all shapes, lengths, and sizes. This is what you need to think about to get going:

You need to get all your information together, as outlined in the previous sections of this chapter. To briefly recap, these are:

1 A list of the competencies, both core and job-related

2 The job description

3 The list of goals and objectives from the last meeting

4 A list of accomplishments

Consider the main points that arise from this information. Think about what the appraisee:

■ Has done well
■ Needs to improve on
■ Needs development on

Prepare to be honest in your assessments and the ratings you give.

Check that any formal written instructions are included with the form when it is given to you by HR.

Although all forms are different, these are the elements common to all of them:

BASIC JOB DATA

This involves the very basic stuff, such as filling in names, payroll numbers, department names, length of time in current job, date of appraisal, and the period covered by appraisal.

RATINGS

An overview of how to use the ratings tool or other measurement method specified on the form, and what each of the ratings scales mean.

JOB RESPONSIBILITIES AND COMPETENCIES

Many forms list the main responsibilities and competencies that an employee is expected to demonstrate. These may include topics such as customer service, teamwork, initiative, productivity, communication, cooperation, problem solving, taking responsibility, punctuality, and attendance, though the list will of course vary from industry to industry. A manager may be asked to circle the appropriate rating on a given scale and/or provide some narrative to go with it. If space is left for narrative, be sure to mention the appraisee's accomplishments as well as any areas where improvement is needed.

Dealing with the form continued

AN ASSESSMENT OF GOALS AND OBJECTIVES

How well did the employee do in achieving set targets and standards? Again, a simple ratings scale may be the only measurement device, or a more narrative style may be called for, or a combination of the two. Again, make sure all achievements are clearly stated. This section may form part of section 3 (see p. 106).

GOALS AND OBJECTIVES FOR THE COMING YEAR

You must think carefully about what to write here. Usually, this is a narrative section, since each employee will require individual assessment. To some extent, new goals will be dictated to you by the needs of the department, perhaps passed down to you from senior management.

In other cases, the appraisal itself will determine what the new goals are, especially if the appraisee is a marginal performer. However, the goals and objectives must be achievable. Nothing is more demotivating for an employee than being set up to fail. We will discuss goal-setting in more detail on pp. 186–189.

FUTURE DEVELOPMENT

How is your employee going to improve? And what areas need greatest attention? This will be a narrative section, which must be honestly and thoughtfully completed. Even good performers will have flaws in some areas, and can improve further in strong areas. It is tempting for managers to skim over this section if the employee is doing fine.

LIST OF MAJOR ACCOMPLISHMENTS

This type of list again forces managers to think hard about what the employee has done (or not done) over the year that is really noteworthy, and will help in making a final, overall assessment.

EMPLOYEE COMMENTS

All employees will have something to say about their performance, and what is expected of them in the year to come. This is the place to voice those opinions, and to sign off on the form. This will also be a narrative part of the form.

OVERALL SUMMARY AND RATING

Many forms provide space for a narrative detailing the employee's overall performance and a brief recap of strengths and weaknesses. Sometimes a final rating is needed.

SIGNATURES

The manager, employee, and manager's supervisor are often required to sign off on the form.

Dealing with the form continued

SOME POINTS TO CONSIDER WHEN FILLING IN THE FORM:

1 Remember to be objective and honest. The form may be used to assess promotions and pay raises and to defend against lawsuits.

2 Whatever the norm in your organization, stick to answering the questions on the form. You can add attachments if there are relevant points to be made that are not adequately covered on the form.

3 Be aware that different rating scales may be used for different questions on the form. These can be anything from 2-point scales to 6-point scales, though 5-point scales are most common.

4 Different weights need be attached to different questions on the form. This is only natural. Some key tasks will always be more important than others. It is often best left to the manager (and appraisee if necessary) to decide which are the most important parts of the job. This is a valuable guide for manager and appraisee to show where both should be concentrating their efforts.

5 A recommended distribution of ratings may be required. Managers tend to rate almost everyone as average in their final analysis. To stop this, senior management may require that only a certain number (or percentage) of employees can fall within each number on the rating scale. For example, only 5 percent may be rated as excellent (a 5 on the ratings scale), 25 percent as good (a 4), 50 percent as average (a 3), 15 percent as acceptable (a 2), and 5 percent as poor (a 1).

preparing for the meeting

Premeeting review

THESE ARE THE THINGS YOU NEED TO DO IMMEDIATELY BEFORE STARTING
YOUR PERFORMANCE REVIEW MEETING:

GATHER YOUR INFORMATION AND MATERIALS

We have touched on lots of points to do with the information managers need to take into the meetings with them. These are the most important:

- The appraisal form, as filled in by the manager.

- Any list of accomplishments, or self-assessments, as completed by the appraisee.

- Last year's appraisal form, complete with agreed goals, objectives, and development ideas.

- Hard evidence and substantial argument to back up your assessment of the appraisee's performance.

ARRANGE AN APPROPRIATE TIME TO MEET

Pick a time that is convenient for both parties. This not only means checking your own schedule, but also being sensitive to the schedule of the appraisee. For example, don't arrange the meeting in the middle of a particularly busy week for the appraisee. This will only cause undue pressure and some resentment.

Further, make sure that you schedule in enough time for the meeting. Also make sure that your following appointments are flexible ones that can be rescheduled at a moment's notice, should your performance review run over. Nothing looks worse than a meeting that is cut short because a manager has to leave for another important meeting.

ARRANGE AN APPROPRIATE PLACE TO MEET

Although most managers end up conducting performance reviews in their offices, some meetings may be better conducted on neutral ground, perhaps even out of the office. Clearly this will be the case if the manager's office is not private, for example, if it is only a cubicle and co-workers can overhear the conversation. In this case, make sure that you book another room in the building or choose another appropriate venue such as a quiet and familiar coffee shop. Ensure wherever you choose is well-lit (but not glaringly bright), heated or air-conditioned, and adequately furnished. Also ensure that you will not be interrupted either by phone calls or people coming into the room. This means informing other staff members such as your PA that a performance appraisal is taking place.

Last, arrange the furniture so that you do not come across as the judge sitting behind the desk. Side-by-side meetings, or meetings with just the edge of the desk between manager and appraisee, are becoming more popular as they create less confrontational body language. On the other hand, sitting behind a desk in an office is a good idea if the appraisee needs to be told that his performance must improve, as the manager must appear to be a figure in control and in authority.

preparing for the meeting

Premeeting review continued

DETERMINE THE AGENDA
Decide on your opening lines. These should establish some rapport. Ideas of what to say are given on pp. 100–103. Then decide how you want the discussion to progress. Tell the appraisee what the agenda is going to be, or perhaps discuss it with him. A typical agenda may look like this:

1 Review work performance, looking at agreed upon objectives

2 Give praise, encouragement, and constructive feedback

3 Assess development success

4 Agree to new objectives

5 Agree to new areas for development

6 Agree to an action plan

7 Appraisee's and manager's final comments

8 Summarize agreed points

SHOW THE APPRAISEE THE COMPLETED FORM IN ADVANCE

Let the appraisee have time to review what you have written about them before the meeting starts. Do this about two hours beforehand. This gives them the chance to consider, in their own time, the manager's conclusions.

However, do not show a poor performer the form beforehand— antagonizing a poor performer before he even comes into the office is not a good idea.

PRACTICE THE MEETING

Just as you would for a job interview, practice aloud all the things you are going to say, and how you are going to say them. This includes all the things you are going to say to build rapport, your body language, and your confident manner. Also practice your answers to the questions you can guess that your appraisee is likely to ask. This will help build your own confidence and smooth the progress of the meeting.

What should an employee consider before her appraisal meeting?

Pages 116–125 deal with recommendations for the appraisee.

No employee should attempt the meeting without preparation. You will be asked searching questions on areas of success and failure that will require full and detailed responses.

BEFORE THE MEETING, YOU SHOULD ASSESS:

1 Your overall, general personal performance over the year.

2 A more detailed assessment of your performance, as measured against the goals and objectives set in the last meeting.

3 If a self-assessment is required in advance of the meeting, send the form (or a list of accomplishments) to your manager, as required by the appraisal process.

4 Any changes that you consider need to be made to the original list of goals and objectives and your job description.

5 Identify where you think your greatest development and training needs lie.

6 Prepare for the face-to-face meeting by deciding on language, style, and tone.

Ideally, your manager will provide guidelines on how to address these issues. If your manager has not provided them, ask for guidance.

preparing for the meeting

Getting the right information before your appraisal meeting

Before you set foot in the appraisal meeting, you must do your homework. You will be asked lots of searching questions, expected to fully participate, and asked to justify your actions. Also, because performance is linked to pay, a good performance meeting may pay dividends in terms of your pay raise.

TO START, COMPILE THIS INFORMATION ABOUT YOURSELF:

1 Your job description

2 Your salary details

3 Your employment record—if you have an up-to-date resumé, this is an ideal place to start

4 Your formal qualifications

All this information will serve to show you where you have been, what you have done, where you are now, what is expected of you in your job, and what the wider aims of your company are.

5 Your training history

6 Previous appraisal forms

7 The list of competencies that you are expected to demonstrate (see pp. 86–87)

8 Your organization's mission statement, values, and vision

Your role as an employee

There are three main issues for you to consider when it comes to an assessment of your role.

YOU MUST:

1 Consider your job

2 Consider your performance

3 Consider your future

CONSIDER YOUR JOB
Ask yourself these questions and note down the answers:

■ What is the primary purpose of my job? Look at your job description to start with.

■ What sort of experience, skills, and qualifications are needed to successfully do my job? Think about your training and the on-the-job experience you have gained over the years.

■ What competencies do I need to show? Find out the core competencies as published by your company, as well as the job-based ones.

▓ How has my job changed?
Consider how your industry has
changed over the years (it
never stands still). Also, think
about the change in internal
departmental reorganizations.

▓ How would my department be
affected if I did not do my job?
Think about what you bring to
the team or department that
would be missed if your job
did not exist.

CONSIDER YOUR PERFORMANCE
Again, think about the answers to
these questions. You will be
expected to discuss the following
issues in the appraisal meeting:

▓ What are your successes over
the past year? This may well be
handled by a self-assessment
or list of accomplishments, so
be specific and honest. You will
be expected to quantify your
claims and show the benefit to
the department and company
as a whole.

■ Where are the areas for improvement? This is often not handled on the self-assessment form, so you will have to be honest about yourself. Again, be specific and give examples, stating what went wrong and, importantly, how you would handle things differently in the future.

■ What standards have you maintained? Think about quality issues, deadlines, and budgets. Ultimately, a company will go a long way to being successful if it can deliver a quality product, on time and on budget. What has your contribution to this been?

■ What parts of your job do you enjoy? Everyone likes and dislikes parts of their job; often, the less palatable parts are the ones that get neglected and suffer in performance terms.

■ What obstacles have you overcome this year? Think about your problem-solving skills and back them up with examples. Conversely, think about the issues that have made your job easier. How could these be built on?

■ What has this year taught you? Think about what you can do now that you couldn't a year ago, and how the skills and experience you gained this year can be built on for next year.

CONSIDER YOUR FUTURE

Once the "here and now" has been discussed, you will be expected to discuss where you see your job and career heading. You may have already touched on this in your job interview.

■ Where do you want to be in three years' time? In 10 years' time? Consider the avenues you would like to explore in your current industry.

■ What do you see as your next job? Consider the stepping-stones that will take you on this career path.

■ What are the obstacles that you will encounter in your career? Think about your skills and training requirements over the coming years.

■ What do you need to overcome the problems you face daily in your current job? Think about the specific training and development you need to do your job better.

■ What help can the department or organization provide you with? This can come from your manager, a mentor, co-workers, or HR.

■ What extra responsibilities do you think you can take on? This is both a developmental question and a question about what will challenge and motivate you over the coming year.

Appraisee checklist

It is essential that the appraisee prepares for the meeting. The main idea is to avoid any unpleasant surprises.

SO BEFOREHAND, MAKE SURE THAT YOU:

1

AGREE ON A CONVENIENT TIME
Try to steer your manager away from conducting a performance review when you are particularly busy.

2

HAVE SEEN A COPY OF THE APPRAISAL
This will enable you to read what has been written about you in good time and will give you fair warning of what will be discussed.

3

HAVE COMPLETED ANY LIST OF ACCOMPLISHMENTS
This will cast you in a good light right from the word go and will focus your mind on how you view your own performance over the past year.

4

ARE CLEAR ABOUT WHAT IS BEING ASSESSED
Find out from your manager what criteria are being used to judge you and the competencies and parts of your job you will be assessed on.

5 HAVE QUESTIONS AND COMMENTS
Prepare your questions and comments thoroughly. You will be expected to participate in a two-way conversation, so you must have something constructive to say. This also means thinking clearly about what you regard as your development, training, and future career needs and plans.

6 UNDERSTAND THE PROCESS
Make sure you understand the whole annual process used by your company, what it is designed to achieve, which parts come when, and your role and involvement in all of them. This will require an explanatory meeting with your manager and a company-led induction course. In addition, many companies will have an appeals process for appraisees who think that their appraisal was unfair. During the meeting, bear this in mind.

7 PRACTICE YOUR BEHAVIOR
You will be expected to conduct yourself like a mature adult. This means giving full, honest answers, listening without interrupting, and not becoming defensive or monosyllabic in the face of feedback that you may not like. Also practice your body language. Maintain an open, neutral face, keep good eye contact (but don't stare), and sit upright with your hands in your lap and your feet on the floor.

in the meeting

What is the purpose of the meeting?

The performance review meeting has two functions, to review the past year's achievements and to set new goals and objectives for the coming year.

1 The appraisee's performance over the past year is discussed and assessed.

2 An assessment is made of how well last year's development plan worked.

3 The appraisal form is the tool used to make this assessment.

4 Any training needs are discussed and may be included in the action plan.

5 New goals and objectives are agreed on for the coming year. If this does not take place in the meeting, it can also happen in a follow-up meeting scheduled for a time when the appraisee has had an opportunity to absorb the performance review.

6 A new development plan is put in place, taking into account the success or otherwise of last year's plan.

7 An action plan is agreed on for putting new targets and plans into work.

8 A system for monitoring progress may be agreed on.

Managers' responsibilities

The manager must conduct the meeting in a professional manner, in accordance with the preparation detailed on pp. 112–115. She must also set the agenda, tone, and timeframe for all the components to be discussed.

THESE ARE THE MANAGER'S RESPONSIBILITIES:

1
Conduct the performance review using the appraisal form and the self-assessment (or list of accomplishments) completed by the appraisee. This is the key point of the meeting. Managers must make sure that they have all the information and evidence they need to back up their conclusions (see pp. 98–99).

2
Explain the appraisee's performance, basing the assessment on the strengths and accomplishments the appraisee has shown, the weaknesses and less successful areas of the appraisee's performance, and the development and training needs that will either drive their performance forward or help correct weaknesses. An action plan is also a useful tool for putting plans into work.

3
Ensure that new goals, objectives, and development plans for the coming appraisal period are fully understood and agreed upon.

4 Make sure that the main conclusions from the meeting are fully understood and will be acted on. Ultimately, this is what will live on after all the other subjects discussed in the meeting have faded.

5 Respond to the appraisee's feedback. Because the appraisal is a two-way conversation, it is essential that managers must learn how to listen to the appraisee's thoughts and reactions. The appraisal process will leave the appraisee in no doubt as to what the manager thinks, but for the meeting to be a success, both parties need come to a mutual understanding of the appraisee's performance. This means that the manager must actively listen (see pp. 135–136) to the appraisee.

6 Deal with the relevant paperwork. This means getting the appraisee to add her comments to the appraisal form, giving details of the appeal process, and getting the form signed off by the manager, the appraisee, and, if necessary, the manager's supervisor.

Creating a positive atmosphere

The manager's job is not to be judge and executioner. It is to provide a useful, informative appraisal that will motivate the appraisee to contribute to greater levels of performance. On the practical side of assessing performance, the manager must also motivate and encourage. This is best done if the atmosphere of the meeting is positive and upbeat.

BE CLEAR ABOUT CONFIDENTIALITY

Many of the issues you will be discussing will appear on the appraisal form and will, therefore, be seen by senior managers and HR. There may well be other matters to discuss that should be kept confidential. Agree in advance which issues these will be, and stick to them. This will earn you immediate respect and encourage the appraisee to open up and be honest with you.

PUT YOURSELF IN THE APPRAISEE'S SHOES

Take a few moments to put yourself in the appraisee's position. How is she likely to be feeling, especially if she has read the appraisal form beforehand? This will help put both of you on the same wavelength.

BE HONEST, CONSISTENT, AND FAIR

Creating a positive atmosphere does not mean that you should avoid talking about difficult issues because this will negate the whole point of the appraisal process. In fact, employees usually appreciate constructive candor. If your approach is open and fair, you will earn respect, even if your message is unpalatable to the appraisee.

SET UP THE ROOM

We have already touched on this (see p. 113). You can make the room feel less confrontational and more comfortable with a little thought. Sitting side-by-side or using the corner of the desk will make you look less like the big bad boss. Clear any clutter away, and make sure your desk is tidy. This will be noticed by the appraisee and will show her that you are making a genuine effort to make her feel at ease.

INTRODUCE THE SESSION

Getting the meeting off to a good start will set the tone for the rest of it. Try to build the appraisee's confidence and reduce her nervousness by stressing the motivational aim of the meeting and by asking an easy question to start with. Don't launch straight into difficult areas. This can be very intimidating.

EXPLAIN THE PURPOSE OF THE MEETING

Explaining what the appraisal meeting is supposed to achieve and what the advantages are for the appraisee creates the right atmosphere. So explain the agenda for the meeting (if you haven't shown it to the appraisee already), and be prepared to listen to and answer any questions the appraisee might have.

Make it a two-way conversation

The appraisal meeting is not just a monologue emanating from the manager. For the meeting to really be a success, the conversation needs to flow. The appraisee must be encouraged to speak and share her views. While this may not be a problem for more extroverted appraisees, or for those anticipating a favorable review, those less inclined to speak will need encouraging. These are the techniques to use:

START WITH AN OPEN ENDED QUESTION

These questions encourage a detailed response. They are the opposite of closed questions, which only encourage a "Yes" or "No" answer. Open-ended questions often start with "Who," "What," "When," "How," and "Where."

THESE ARE SOME EXAMPLES:

1 "How do you think procedure could be improved?"

2 "What do you regard as the most important issue here?"

3 "Where can costs be cut without affecting quality?"

All of these questions invoke a response that is more than just a single word answer. Avoid using "Why" as this implies you are demanding an explanation and sounds accusatory, even if you do not mean it to. Instead, use such phrases as "What are the reasons for . . . " or "How do you understand the situation regarding . . . ?"

LISTEN ACTIVELY

All conversations work on the premise that one person speaks, the other listens and then responds, while the first speaker listens to that response. However, in practice, we all spend a lot of time interrupting, being distracted, second-guessing what the speaker is going to say, finishing sentences for them, and formulating answers before we've heard them out. This may be fine while chatting with friends but not in important work situations.

Ironically, listening properly, or "actively," is a key way to encourage people to talk. It means:

■ Listening in a thoughtful and attentive way, clearly paying attention to what is being said. This is signaled by an engaged expression on your face. It means keeping an open, neutral face and not staring blankly into the middle distance.

■ Maintaining eye contact. This signals complete attention. Looking at the floor, at your notes, or over the appraisee's shoulder shows you're not really listening.

Make it a two-way conversation continued

■ Not fidgeting or being distracted. Playing with your pen or your notes or picking bits of fluff off your suit while the appraisee is talking should be avoided. Again it shows that you're not really interested.

■ Gently nodding your head at key points. Physically acknowledging that you have heard what is being said is a clear sign that you are paying attention.

■ Not interrupting. Listening properly means hearing the other person out and not second-guessing what they are going to say.

■ Briefly summarizing what has just been said. It shows you have been paying attention and want to be clear that you fully understand what you have just been told. This is sometimes called "reflective" listening.

All of these strategies will demonstrate that you are genuinely and sincerely interested in what is being said to you. This is very encouraging for the appraisee and will pass a clear signal that you are worth making the effort to open up to.

RESPECT DIFFERENCES OF OPINION

A two-way conversation entails two people expressing different points of view. You may hear things that you had not previously thought of. Be open to having your mind changed. Even if you don't agree with a particular point of view, you must respect the appraisee's right to have an opinion. This will encourage the appraisee to open up. Avoid loudly cutting her short or dismissing her standpoint as this will have the opposite effect.

Bear in mind, however, that you must reserve the right to disagree—as the manager you must have the courage of your convictions. Say something like "I can see where you're coming from, but I don't think that you have arrived at the right conclusion." Then go on to explain why. If no agreement is reached, leave it at that, and move on.

Feedback do's and don'ts

We have looked at the principles of feedback in chapter 2 (see pp. 46–47), but what should you say? Here are some examples:

DO:

1

START WITH THE POSITIVES
After you have welcomed the appraisee in and have broken the ice, find something in the appraisal form that shows good performance. Unless you are dealing with a very poor performer (see pp. 226–229 for dealing with performance problems), you will find something to say. This gets the appraisal off to an upbeat start. Say something like: "Last year, you exceeded the sales target we set by 10 percent. In the face of deteriorating industry conditions, this is exceptional performance."

2

DESCRIBE OBSERVABLE BEHAVIORS
Draw your conclusions on nonquantifiable aspects of performance on specific behaviors. Don't say, "It's great that you always seem available to help out." Instead say something like: "When I needed assistance in rescheduling Project X, you ensured that the deadline for the new plan was met by routinely taking on extra tasks."

DON'T:

1

BE A SHOW-OFF

Just because you are the manager it doesn't mean that you can come across as a know-it-all, patronize the appraisee, or use your seniority to dismiss what the appraisee is saying. This will immediately irritate the appraisee and cause her to clam up.

2

TALK INCESSANTLY

An appraisal is a two-way conversation, so don't use the meeting as an excuse to get on your soap box and take over the conversation. This will look as though you don't care what the appraisee thinks or has to say.

3

ANSWER YOUR OWN QUESTIONS

Allow the appraisee time to answer your questions. Avoid hurrying her along by quickly interjecting with your own answer. This is very off-putting and negates the idea that feedback is a two-way process.

4

ACCENTUATE THE NEGATIVE

If you have to give negative feedback—and under no circumstances should you be afraid to do so when the situation demands it—choose your words carefully and with sensitivity.

Reading nonverbal signs

Communication does not come exclusively from what people say. Their body language and general reactions also say a great deal about how they are feeling and what they are thinking.

LOOK FOR THESE SIGNS TO GAUGE NEGATIVE NON-VERBAL SIGNALS:

CHANGES IN TONE

A tricky subject will probably result in a change in tone of voice. The appraisee will tend to naturally speak confidently when discussing her successes, but her tone of voice will often lower as this confidence falters. Her tone will become flatter and the volume will fall. Her speech will become more faltering and broken as she struggles to find the right words. The effect will be made all the more obvious because she may end up talking to her feet.

CHANGES IN FACIAL EXPRESSION

As the appraisee starts to falter, her facial expressions may change. Eye contact may break at a particular point, and her eyes may dart about. This may be accompanied by a slight bowing of the head. This will indicate that perhaps the appraisee is not being totally honest with you. Also, the eyes may disengage and start to stare into the middle distance. An open, receptive face may quickly become closed and tense around the forehead and the jaw.

CHANGES IN POSTURE
The appraisal meeting may be going smoothly but then moves onto a topic that causes the appraisee to stop talking. Quick changes in posture are often indicative of agitation and concern. These might include:

1 Suddenly stiffening in posture.

2 Suddenly crossing her arms and legs. This is a defensive posture.

3 Suddenly sitting back in her chair and crossing her hands. This indicates reluctance.

4 Clenching her fists.

Reading nonverbal signs continued

5 Shifting to sit on the edge of her chair. This indicates nervousness and anxiety.

6 Diverting attention away from you and to the floor or a point over your shoulder.

7 Taking a sharp breath, or a sigh.

This will indicate that the topic is a difficult one for the appraisee to deal with, and one she would perhaps rather gloss over.

If you see reactions such as these, acknowledge them. Make sure you keep asking open questions to get to the bottom of the causes of her agitation or discomfort. After all, no one can improve if less successful parts of their performance are just glossed over. Say something like: "I can see that you're very worried about my assessment of your customer service skills. Why is this?" and then go on to explain to the appraisee why you have arrived at your conclusion and later, how you suggest the problem be remedied.

Once you have noted these anxieties and gotten to the bottom of them, try to get the meeting back onto a positive footing by doing the following:

ADOPT THE RIGHT POSTURE

If you adopt the right posture, this will encourage the appraisee to relax as well. Try to maintain an open posture, with your hands in your lap. Avoid crossing your arms and legs as this puts up a barrier between you and the appraisee. Also do not lean on your desk or slouch in your chair as both of these will suggest a nonneutral pose.

FACIAL EXPRESSIONS

Your own facial expressions are just as important as your ability to read the appraisee's face. Use an open smile, engaged eye contact, relaxed face (no frowns, grimaces, or shocked looks), and a steady head position.

Practice sitting in an open posture and controlling your facial expressions so you do not have to think about them during the meeting. You can influence the appraisee's posture by getting your own posture right yourself, whereby the appraisee's body language mirrors the manager's. When this happens, both parties are in rapport, and the meeting will be conducted in a positive atmosphere. By adopting a relaxed but alert posture, managers can encourage appraisees to mirror their positive body language.

Dealing with performance problems

Clearly, managers' lives would be made much easier if all appraisees were outstanding performers and all the manager had to do was heap on the praise and encourage further success. Indeed, in many cases, appraisees' performance is at least acceptable, but there will be some cases in which you have to deal with poor performers.

THE CAUSES OF POOR PERFORMANCE:

1

PROBLEM An inability to do the job as described in the job description and the list of competencies, as a result of lack of experience or an error in appointing or promoting the wrong person.

SOLUTION Provide on-the-job training and support. If the wrong person has been employed, consider offering a transfer to a more suitable role.

2

PROBLEM Lack of training. This includes a lack of essential skills or job-based knowledge.

SOLUTION Identify gaps in skills and knowledge. This is best done with the participation of the appraisee. Suggest development activities and training ideas to bring the appraisee up to speed.

3

PROBLEM Lack of motivation, due to boredom or lack of a challenge. Conversely, too much of a challenge can also demotivate. Why even try when you know you can't succeed?

SOLUTION Review the tasks that form the appraisee's job. Suggest new areas in which the appraisee could become involved to provide a new challenge and a new interest. Conversely, review the workload the appraisee is expected to meet, and consider delegating some of it elsewhere, if necessary.

4

PROBLEM Lack of concentration. Is there an outside or personal problem claiming the employee's attention?

SOLUTION Gently inquire as to what the real problem is. Stress that this will remain confidential, and agree time off so that the problem can be dealt with. Suggest professional help if performance does not pick up.

5

PROBLEM Lack of involvement in either the team, department, or organization as a whole. This can lead to alienation.

SOLUTION Encourage new roles, such as becoming more involved in staff meetings, or joining the social events team. These can bring help people back into the fold. A career counselor may also be able to help.

Tips for dealing with the appraisee

Deal with any challenges that arise immediately. You must remain in charge and retain your credibility.

Tell the appraisee right at the start of the meeting that you think that her performance is substandard. This gets the issue out in the open right away and encourages discussion of the problem after the appraisee has had a chance to read the appraisal form.

Gain acknowlegment that a problem exists. If the appraisee remains in denial, then nothing can be done to remedy her performance. If you get her to admit that a problem does exist, then you will be able to take the first steps in dealing with it constructively by identifying causes and asking the appraisee what she thinks should be done. To gain acknowledgment, explain how her poor performance has affected that of the team or the organization. Ensure that she fully understands where she has gone wrong and the consequences for the business of allowing their poor performance to continue. Encourage the employee to reflect on what you have said.

If the employee disagrees with a part of your assessment, make sure you have the facts that led you to your conclusion on hand. This is the evidence you need to gather before the start of the meeting (see pp. 112). It is usually quite clear where areas of disagreement will crop up, so make sure you have some answers on hand. Use active listening and open questions to get to the root of the problem. Your primary aim in this type of situation is to gain the employee's understanding, not her agreement.

Be specific about what the problem is. You will have to state what the difference is between the performance you require and the actual performance you have noted. Being completely transparent is very important. If an employee is often late for work, don't say "You're always late for work." Instead, say "You are expected to be ready to start work at 9:00 A.M. each day. This week you have arrived at 9:25, 9:10, and 9:15. On Thursday you were on time, which was good. I would like you to continue to be on time, every day."

Dealing with emotional reactions

For the most part, poorly performing appraisees may be disappointed that you have rated them badly, but there will be times when the bad news provokes a strong emotional reaction.

THESE ARE THE SITUATIONS YOU MAY FACE, AND HOW TO DEAL WITH THEM:

1 SUBMISSIVENESS
BEHAVIOR
The appraisee looks away, and perhaps turns her body away. By metaphorically lying down, she is exhibiting what behaviorists call a flight reaction. Submission helps her to run from the situation. To make it easier to flee, she may actually agree with what is being said, even though it is clear she is only doing so to bring the conversation to a close as quickly as possible. Her voice may become quieter and deliberately nonconfrontational.

YOUR REACTION
Don't accept platitudes at face value. It is very easy to just agree and move on to avoid an embarrassing situation. Keep asking open questions to get to the bottom of why her performance was bad, and make sure that there is a genuine commitment to change. This is much more important than just gaining simple acknowledgment that her performance was poor.

2

ANGER
BEHAVIOR
By contrast, anger is a type of fight reaction. In this instance, the appraisee has decided to battle her way out. This inevitably involves a raised level of aggression, which manifests itself as an angry, raised voice, a defiant posture, perhaps some finger pointing, or lots of arm and hand movements.

YOUR REACTION
Remain calm and think very carefully about what you are going to say. Behaving in the opposite way to the appraisee will cool things off. Reacting angrily will only increase the temperature further. Listen to the appraisee's grievances, denials, or excuses, and ask for examples of where her opinion differs from yours.

Pointing out the appraisee's anger is often enough to get her to modify her tone. Ultimately, anger has no real place in a business meeting, so do not be afraid to ask her to behave more professionally. If the appraisee still continues to shout, tell her you will abort the meeting, and, if necessary, leave the room. You must report this to your supervisor and HR. There is a potential disciplinary situation here.

Dealing with emotional reactions continued

3 TEARS

BEHAVIOR

The appraisee gets so upset that she bursts into tears. This is because either the terrible truth about her performance has suddenly been brought out into the open, she can't believe the injustice of your assessment, or she is trying to win your sympathy. Whatever the reason, it is extremely unsettling to have this happen.

YOUR REACTION

A box of tissues is a useful prop here! Make sure you have some to hand. As with the anger situation, remain calm, and allow the appraisee to compose herself. Very often, tears are a result of shock, so the meeting can usually continue once the shock has passed. Do not let tears stop you from getting your point across—what you had intended to say is no less valid, and must still be said.

As with anger, if the appraisee cannot collect herself and behave in a professional, business-like manner, you must tell her that the meeting will be aborted unless she stops crying. If no change occurs, abort the meeting. Again, report the matter to your supervisor and HR.

4 VIOLENCE

BEHAVIOR

Some appraisees may become so angry that their reactions become physical, or they deliberately seek to intimidate with threatening behavior or verbal abuse.

YOUR REACTION

Clearly, this is the worst possible situation of all because your well-being is at risk. Get up and leave immediately, without any preamble.

The only managerial skill you can employ here is to try to spot the potential for violence before the meeting starts. If you have seen the employee losing her temper over trivial matters, bragging about fights she has been in, or exhibiting any intimidating behavior, then these are the signs that a confrontation may occur. If this is the case, then perhaps consider whether a performance appraisal is suitable at all.

If you do decide to go ahead, first find out whether you have an emergency plan in force at your company for dealing with violent staff. In some states, plans like these are a legal requirement. Alternatively, have someone watching your office discreetly. This is most likely to be a member of your security staff. Sit by the door so you can make an quick exit should the situation demand it.

Obviously, any violence or threat of violence is unacceptable and must be reported immediately to your supervisor. The appraisee must be immediately fired and ejected from the building. Depending on your company policy, call the police as well.

Dealing with the money issue

The purpose of the appraisal meeting is to review performance, set goals and objectives for the coming period, and assess development needs. Even though performance is related to pay at many companies, the meeting itself is not the place to talk about a pay raise.

This is because performance is not the only factor in determining pay. Also, if the appraisal is seen by the appraisee as an obstacle that needs to be overcome in order to win a pay raise, then the appraisee is likely to be defensive and not honest about performance.

First, make sure that you follow company policy with respect to discussing money in the meeting. If policy means you should not broach the subject, make sure that the appraisee is aware of this before the meeting. Then you can say something like: "I would like our meeting today to concentrate on assessing performance. It is not company policy to discuss pay raises in performance review meetings, and this is enforced company-wide. However, you should be aware that this company does link performance to pay, so once we have finished our discussion I will fix a time with you to discuss your pay raise."

If this is not the culture at your company, and it is customary to talk about pay raises in the meeting, get it out of the way at the very start, before you start reviewing the appraisal form. This ensures that the appraisee does not spend the meeting wondering how much she is going to get at the end of it. Say something like: "Your pay raise this year will be 3 percent. This is in line with other staff members who have received similar performance ratings." Then go on to start the meeting proper.

SOME USEFUL PHRASES

1 "As you know, it is company policy not to discuss remuneration at an appraisal meeting."

2 "I will be discussing pay rises with HR when I have completed the appraisal process for the whole team."

3 "We are looking at salary and benefits packages, and will be talking to staff shortly."

4 "I intend to focus only on your performance in this meeting."

5 "Your major successes this year have been . . . ."

Dealing with extenuating circumstances

During the performance review, you may discover that the appraisee has severe problems outside of the workplace that are distracting her from carrying out her tasks effectively. She could be going through a divorce, has elderly and sick parents, or is ill. So how do you deal with it?

You must be balanced in your aims as a manager. First, it is very important to empathize with the appraisee, and, no doubt, life events such as the ones described here are terrible for anyone to go through. However, you must realize the role of the performance review—to assess performance. This means that you cannot alter your assessment—you must tell the truth or the whole process loses its integrity. It is not your role to say that a poor performer can be excused because of circumstance.

In the meeting, gently point out the areas where performance has suffered. Most importantly, discuss and draw up a detailed recovery plan to get the employee back on track. This may include taking some time off work to deal with the problem, followed by regular follow-up meetings to see how matters are progressing, both in and out of work. You must insist that you are kept informed of progress. If the problem continues, it is inevitable that your supervisor and HR will need to be informed. Do this in good time as continuing poor performance or absence from work will undoubtedly be covered by company policy.

You may have noticed a deterioration in the appraisee's performance long before the appraisal meeting itself. This may be particularly marked if the appraisee is usually a strong performer. As soon as you see this deterioration, have a quiet word to find out what is wrong. You may be able to rescue the situation before appraisal time comes around and you find yourself having to rate her as a poor performer. It may also encourage the appraisee to start taking steps toward resolving out-of-work problems if her performance has been spotted and brought out into the open quickly. It will also ensure that there are no nasty surprises for either of you during the performance review meeting.

Language to use

Here are some suggestions for what to say in the appraisal meeting.

STARTING THE MEETING

1

GREET YOUR EMPLOYEE AND SAY WHY YOU'RE MEETING
"Hello John, come in and sit down. Did you see the game over the weekend? I can't believe Team X lost. Anyway, I'm really pleased we have this opportunity to discuss how things have been going over the past year. This meeting is really important to us both, so I'd like to discuss matters in detail. It should take about an hour."

2

SAY WHERE YOU'RE GOING TO START
"I'd like to start by discussing your self-assessment (or list of accomplishments) and the parts of your job that you think have gone well this year. Then we'll talk about the appraisal I wrote about you, and which you've had a chance to read."

3

GET GOING
"So, to get going, why don't we look at your self-assessment, and you can tell me what you think has gone well this year."

4 CONTINUE WITH PLAN
"I would like to start by looking at your job description and competencies and then see how you got on with the goals and objectives we set last year. Then we'll set goals and objectives for the coming year, devise an action plan to implement them, and then review your job description."

5 DISCUSS OVERALL RATINGS
"I will then give you my final rating of your work and explain why I have come to this conclusion."

6 CONDUCT THE DISCUSSION
"Let's talk about the areas that have gone well, then look at areas that can be improved, the reasons why, and how to make things better. I would like to talk, then we can discuss where you agree with me, and where you don't. We will both have a chance to give our point of view."

7 GET A REACTION
"Overall, what are your initial thoughts on your achievements over the past year?" Then ask, "How do you see your weaker areas in light of our discussion?"

Language to use continued

As with the rest of the meeting, close your discussions with clarity, and on a positive note, with future actions clear to both parties.

CLOSING THE MEETING

1

SUMMARIZE THE DISCUSSION
"OK, that just about wraps things up. Just to go over what we've discussed, these are the key points I would like to you to take on board." The key points should be concise and contain the main message you are trying to get across.

2

BE CLEAR ABOUT AREAS TO BE IMPROVED
"Your performance could be improved in the following areas (briefly state what these areas are). Sales in the third quarter started to fall as you lost focus on customer service."

3

REINFORCE AREAS OF SUCCESS
"Your performance has been particularly good in the following areas (briefly state what these areas are). You have done well here because you took the initiative at an early stage, and it really paid dividends. You also avoided potential distribution problems by outsourcing some of our warehousing."

4 COMPLETE THE PAPERWORK
"I would like you to now sign the appraisal form showing that you've read and discussed it with me. You can also add any extra comments if you wish."

5 BE CLEAR ABOUT GOALS, OBJECTIVES, AND DEVELOPMENT PLANS
"We agreed that your goals and objectives are to increase sales by 5 percent and to increase your customer focus by delegating more of the administrative work. We also agreed that you would visit two conferences a year to build a wider client base."

6 BUILD IN AN OPPORTUNITY FOR THE APPRAISEE TO RESPOND
"Do you fully understand what we have discussed today and what your role is over the coming period? I hope I have managed to explain myself clearly. What do you think?"

7 THANK THE APPRAISEE AND LOOK FORWARD
"Thank you for your input and involvement. This has been a really useful discussion. We will meet again in a week for the follow-up meeting (if one is planned) to review your reaction to this review."

in the meeting

Appraisees' responsibilities

Pages 160–183 deal with recommendations for the employee.

Just as the manager has to handle the meeting successfully, the appraisee (and the manager when being appraised) must also take responsibility for it going well. Knowing what to do and say are vital if the appraisee is to make the most of the meeting.

THE APPRAISEE NEEDS TO:

1

BE PREPARED TO TALK ABOUT THE SELF-ASSESSMENT (OR LIST OF ACCOMPLISHMENTS)

This is a useful tool for ensuring that your achievements are highlighted and discussed. Reread your list and be ready to say what you have done that was so impressive and why, with particular reference to your goals and development plan set in last year's meeting.

2

BE PREPARED TO DISCUSS DIFFERENCES BETWEEN THE SELF-ASSESSMENT AND YOUR MANAGER'S ASSESSMENT

You must think about where your manager might disagree with your self-assessment. For example, you know you missed your sales target, which is likely to be thought of by your manager as a problem, but you feel you still did an outstanding job considering the worsening market conditions. This discussion should also take place even when performance is good. Be prepared to come to an understanding.

3 BE PREPARED TO ASK QUESTIONS

This is critical. Your manager will expect considerable feedback from you during the meeting. Remember, this is a two-way process. You, too, can use open questions to clarify why a certain rating has been given for an area of your performance. Also, do not be afraid to ask for examples to illustrate why your manager has arrived at a certain conclusion.

4 BE PREPARED TO RESPOND CALMLY TO CRITICISM

Even if you feel your manager is not assessing you accurately, remember that you are in a business meeting. This means that you must be prepared to state your point of view in a reasonable tone of voice. There is a maxim that says you can "disagree without being disagreeable."

5 BE PREPARED TO LEARN FROM THE MANAGER'S ATTITUDE

In an ideal world, all deadlines are met, and all goods and services are produced and provided to the highest quality. In reality, one or the other often suffers. Be prepared to learn to address or change your approach to completing projects in line with the criteria your manager uses to assess your performance—for example, quality may be more important than deadlines, whereas you had assumed it to be the other way around.

Understanding your manager when you are appraised

Your manager will be under pressure to achieve results, as specified by her own supervisor. As the manager's subordinate, she will be looking to you, as a member of the department, to play your part in achieving that success.

So it will be helpful for you to put yourself in your manager's shoes and see what she will be looking for. This will also help you see the wider perspective involved in a performance review, and help you to realize that appraisal is not a case of you against your manager. It is a case of you performing to agreed standards so that you contribute fully to overall departmental success.

CONSIDER THE FOLLOWING ISSUES WHEN FRAMING YOUR ANSWERS IN THE APPRAISAL MEETING:

KEY QUESTIONS

1 What targets does my manager need to hit in order for the team or department she is running, and to which I belong, to be considered successful?

2 What gauges will my manager use to assess whether or not she has been successful?

3 What are the criteria that my manager will be assessed on when it is her turn to be appraised?

4 In light of these issues, what are the criteria that my manager will be using to judge my success?

5 What did I do to contribute to this success and how did I do it?

6 What should I do to change my input to contribute further to this success?

KEY QUESTIONS

Dealing with managers' questions

Your manager may not be an expert at posing and articulating the right sort of questions. It is important to realize this because if she is not asking the right questions, you may not have the opportunity to get to say all the things you want to. This is how to get your point across, even if you are not given the chance to do so:

OPEN AND CLOSED QUESTIONS

We have seen that open questions are the best way for both your manager and yourself to invite full and detailed answers. To recap, these questions often start with "How," "What," "When," "Where," and "Who," and avoid a "Yes" or a "No" "closed" response. Inexperienced managers may find it difficult to keep the momentum up and may start asking closed questions. Look out for these; you will have to answer the question as if it were an open one.

For example, if you are asked: "Your deadlines are becoming increasingly hard to meet, aren't they?" don't just answer "Yes." Say something like, "Yes they are, but I believe my time management training is helping relieve some of the pressure. I have also been able to delegate some of my less important tasks to the new sales assistant." This lets your manager know that you are successfully developing two key skills—time management and delegation—that would otherwise have gone unmentioned.

1 "I would like to answer that by talking about . . . ."

BOXED-IN QUESTIONS

In another twist on the closed question scenario, you may be asked a question that tries to box you in by giving you only two options—either/or—where neither is the one you want to choose.

For example, if you are asked: "Do you want to continue working for the subsidiary of Big Bank, Inc., or to move to head office?" when you want to do neither, say something like: "Those two suggestions are interesting, but what I would really like to do is gain specialist experience working in the Asian market."

Maneuver your way out by politely making your real wishes clear.

1 "I would like to take the opportunity at this point to . . . ."

2 "The area that interests me most currently is . . . ."

Dealing with managers' questions continued

RHETORICAL QUESTIONS

Some questions require almost no answer or push you into answering in a certain way. Rhetorical questions do this and are similar to boxed-in questions in that they present only a limited scope for replying.

For example, if you are asked: "You are really pressed for time at the moment, so you need a more powerful computer, don't you?" when what you really need is a new assistant, say something like: "Up-to-date technology is always a help, but what I really need to help me with the new client account is a new assistant."

Politely make clear what you believe the real issue to be; otherwise, it will never be discussed or noted.

1 "Training in using the new software would really help the workflow in the department."

2 "It is becoming more difficult to handle the increased workload with the same number of team members."

3 "IT support would be very useful."

MULTIPLE QUESTIONS

Ideally, you will be asked one open, pertinent question at a time, for which you will give one pertinent answer. However, many managers will ask you several questions in the same breath, covering a range of issues, making it very hard to know which one to answer first or which one is the most important. The trick here is to tease the questions out into individual ones.

For example if you are asked: "Would you like to talk about your training needs? Or how you see your self-development working? Or how more on-the-job training will give you extra experience?" you could say something like: "All of these issues are very important to me, so perhaps I could answer them one at a time."

1 "I would certainly welcome the opportunity to discuss training when we have covered my development goals."

2 "More on-the-job experience would be useful, but I would like to discuss backing that up with a formal training course."

3 "Can we return now to the question of future development?"

Dealing with managerial feedback

As with asking the right type of questions (and avoiding asking the wrong ones), your manager may not give you very effective feedback. In fact, her feedback may sound more like criticism. It is important that you do not take offense or become defensive, and it is even more important that you deal with the situation in such a way as to get the feedback that you need.

THIS IS HOW TO DO IT:

1 Don't interrupt. Listen actively (see pp. 135–136) to what you are being told and wait for your manager to finish speaking.

2 Briefly summarize what your manager has just said. This shows you have been listening and gives you a chance to make sure that you have not misunderstood what has just been said. Nothing sounds worse than refuting your manager's assessment only to find that you've got the wrong end of the stick.

3 Bear in mind that all feedback—properly delivered or not—is valuable guidance on where you have gone wrong. It is important that you listen to the actual content of what is being said, even if the style of delivery leaves much to be desired.

4 Then say why you disagree, giving examples and reasons. Try to stay calm and speak in a clear but reasonable tone. Do not become irritated or outraged.

5 Ask for specific examples from your manager when she is delivering her feedback. This will do much to provide clarity in situations where your manager is being vague.

6 If you receive positive feedback, discuss and understand it in exactly the same way as you would negative feedback. You do not have to be modest about your achievements.

7 Thank your manager for being open with you. Even if the feedback was delivered poorly, you can still extract the real issues from it.

Dealing with an overcritical boss

For the most part, managers do understand that is important to take a genuine interest in the performance and development of their staff, even if they stumble through the performance review process, standing on everyone's toes as they do so.

There will be times, however, when you might feel that your boss is not applying the same objective principles to the appraisal process as you have a right to expect, and is carrying this over into the meeting. What do you do if your manager is being irrationally overcritical, or even worse, bullying or abusing you?

Just as in every other walk of life, bullying is used as a method of control, and coming from your boss, bullying is very effective— no one wants to answer back if the boss is shouting.

This makes the buildup to the meeting very unpleasant because you will be anticipating more of the same treatment.

IF THIS IS YOUR SITUATION, REALIZE THAT:

1 Your boss is behaving unprofessionally.

2 Your boss is harming the company by making staff too afraid to accurately report to him.

3 Your boss is harming the company by demotivating staff. No one wants to work for a bully.

4 Your boss is not taking appraisal seriously. Staff will use every tactic to put the meeting off to avoid a confrontation.

THESE ARE THE TACTICS TO EMPLOY IN THE MEETING WITH A BULLYING BOSS:

1 Do all your paperwork exactly as asked and on time.

2 Be on time for the meeting.

3 Speak clearly and in a reasonable tone.

Dealing with an overcritical boss continued

4 Remain resolutely polite and professional. Although the situation is very unpleasant, try to look at it as good training for dealing with all the other bullies you are likely to encounter in life.

5 Also, simply barking back in the same way as you are being spoken to will only serve to raise the temperature of the meeting further.

6 Being professional means not taking adverse comments personally. Again, tell yourself that this is good training and experience for dealing with tough situations.

7 Listen very carefully, and make sure your answers are well-formulated before you speak. This should be easier if you have prepared well for the meeting.

8 Take a deep breath, and remind yourself that you are the model of professionalism.

9 Do not be afraid to stand up for yourself. It is perfectly acceptable in all appraisal meetings, irrespective of their circumstances, to disagree with the assessments being made about you. The key to successful disagreement is the tone that you adopt. Bear in mind that follow-up meetings are often the best place to voice thoughtful disagreement. Ask for specific examples to clarify your boss's reasoning.

10 You could ask politely, but directly, that your boss please keep her voice down. This is risky, but you are well within your rights to ask that the meeting be conducted in a respectful way.

There may come a time during the meeting when none of these tactics have any effect, and, no matter what you say, your boss becomes increasingly angry or abusive. In this case, recognize that the meeting is over. In fact, continuing to talk will only make things worse and may even jeopardize your future prospects at work. Politely say, "I am in no doubt as to what your assessment is, but I do not agree with it, for the reasons I have just stated" and leave it at that. Then ask to be excused. We will deal with what happens next in the following section.

Dealing with an unfair appraisal

Once the meeting has come to an end (for whatever reason), you may
want to pursue the matter if you genuinely believe that the outcome of
your appraisal is unfair.

1 SIGNING THE FORM AND FURTHER COMMENTS
If you have to leave the meeting quickly, you will obviously not
have had time to sign the appraisal form. Your manager will
expect you to do so, and you will have to do so (remember that
signing the form does not mean you agree with what's written
on it. It means you have read, discussed, and understood its
contents), but you also have the right to add your own
comments, and most forms provide space for you to do so.
  If there is no space on your form, write out your concerns on a
separate sheet and ask for this to be attached to the form as
part of the written appraisal, or put in your personnel folder.

2 GETTING FORMAL ADVICE
Before you make an "official" move, make sure that you make
an appointment with your HR department and discuss the
issue with them. HR should not take sides in these kinds of
disputes and will be able to advise you on official company
policy and procedure in dealing with these kinds of complaints.

3 GETTING ANOTHER OPINION
Unless the appraisal has resulted in termination, taking legal action is an unlikely response. Take some time to consider your options. It is important to investigate informal options, such as the follow-up meeting, before going on record, which can be very counterproductive. You could consider seeking support from another manager whom you know and trust. This manager could act as an impartial mediator between you and your boss or be able to offer you off-the-record advice on how to handle the situation.

4 USING THE APPEAL PROCESS
Many organizations have an appeals process, or grievance procedure policy, to deal with friction between managers and their staff. These are always in-house reviews and are intended to objectivize the problem. You will have to file a formal grievance against your boss that will then be seen by other parties, including your boss's supervisor.

5 BEING PREPARED

It is worth stressing, though, that you must be prepared for a bumpy ride. By the nature of your position, you are the subordinate, and your manager is the boss. This automatically makes you vulnerable. Make sure that your grievance is based solely on fact and that you can fully explain in an objective way why you think the appraisal result was unfair. You cannot hope for any success from a complaints procedure just because you don't get along with your boss.

6 DOING NOTHING

Gauging what action to take is a tough call. In some circumstances, doing nothing may be the best option. Depending on your seniority, you may be able to just dismiss the issue as an irritation that you can put to one side. You might also realize that many bullying bosses end up leaving or being fired as their behavior and its effects come to the attention of senior managers. However, if your boss owns the company, or is a senior figure there, then clearly there is little room for maneuver and any professional relationship might now be impossible.

7 ACTING PROFESSIONALLY
There is little to be done in this circumstance except to keep
your head down. Do everything that is required with
professionalism and good grace. Remember that you do not
have to put up with bullying or aggression, and you should not
be singled out for unpopular assignments. If you feel this is
happening, talk to HR. There may be openings in other
departments, working for a different manager.

8 LOOKING AROUND
Your best recourse in an impossible situation is to look for other
work. Sharpen your resumé, network, sign on with a
recruitment consultant, and generally do everything you can to
secure a new position.

How to disagree

There is always the chance that your assessment of your work and what your development needs are is different from that of your manager. So how do you disagree, get your point across, do it all in the right tone, and still come across as a committed member of staff?

This is the formula that will give you a chance of success, and one that will avoid a disagreement turning into a confrontation. So if your performance in a particular area is judged to be below standard and you believe it was not your fault:

■ Agree that your performance was below par.

■ Say that you understand that it was important that your performance in this area should have been better.

■ Request the chance to explain why you underperformed.

■ Give your reasons, stating what happened.

■ Request acknowledgment of your point of view.

■ Suggest a solution to avoid the problem in the future.

For example, your manager says: "The budget ran out of control on the Big Bank, Inc. advertising campaign, and this put our profitability on this project at risk." Your first reaction might just be to say something defensive like: "It wasn't my fault." This is not a helpful thing to say and is not something your manager is likely to accept as a reason. You need to explain fully what went wrong and why.

Your reply should be something like: "Yes, the budget limits were greatly exceeded. I know that the margins on this project were tight and that this made budget control very important. I would like the opportunity to explain what went wrong. First, the photoshoots took much longer to complete than expected due to a shortage of models. Then, the post-production requirements were increased by the client. I hope you can see that these problems were beyond my control. In the future, it would be very helpful if I was present at the meeting where the budget is set so I can anticipate any problems in advance."

Assessing your own performance

After you leave the meeting, go somewhere and relax for a while, no matter how well or badly it went. Once you have had a chance to recover, do not treat the appraisal as an unpleasant experience over for another year and forget about it. Ideally, you should learn from the meeting, so next year you can perform better.

ANSWER THESE QUESTIONS TO SEE WHERE THINGS WENT WELL OR BADLY:

KEY QUESTIONS

1 Did I take the appraisal seriously and realize its importance?

2 Did I prepare adequately for the meeting?

3 Did I make sure I understood and completed the paperwork?

4 Did I present my accomplishments in the best light?

5 Did I rate my overall performance honestly in all the main parts of my job?

6 Did I speak clearly about my job and career plans?

7 Did I speak in a calm, assured, and reasonable tone throughout the meeting?

8 Was my body language appropriate?

9 Did I employ the skills of active listening?

KEY QUESTIONS

10 Did I employ the skills of dealing with questions and feedback?

11 Did I play a full and active part in making the discussion a two-way conversation?

12 Did I offer helpful suggestions and constructive feedback to my manager?

13 Did I fully explain and expand on my key achievements/reasons for failure?

14 Was I prepared to discuss areas for improvement without getting defensive?

15 Did I know where my training needs were?

16 Did I know how to discuss my development needs?

17 Did I appreciate where my skills and experience were strong/ found wanting?

18 Did I know where my job could be improved?

19 Could I suggest areas for taking on more responsibility?

20 Did I understand my manager's point of view?

KEY QUESTIONS

setting new objectives

How to set goals and objectives

As with all other parts of the appraisal system, both the manager and the appraisee have their part to play in setting goals and objectives. But how do you know which ones to set and which ones to prioritize?

CONSIDER THESE POINTS:

1

WHAT IS THE COMPANY'S MISSION STATEMENT?
Take this as your starting point, because, overall, everyone should be working toward the broader values and vision set by senior management. What should the appraisee be doing to achieve this vision?

2

DO I HAVE A LIST OF COMPETENCIES?
These will be core competencies (that everyone in the company is expected to demonstrate), and job-based competencies (the behaviors that are attached to individual roles) (see pp. 86–87). Both are important guides to the types of goals you need to set. As with the company's mission statement, the goals and objectives you set here should aim to get the appraisee working toward these competencies.

3 WHAT ARE THE TASKS SET OUT IN THE APPRAISEE'S JOB DESCRIPTION?
The job description should help you specify key areas where
most effort needs to be directed, even if the description itself is
not very good (see pp. 94–97 on job descriptions).

4 DO I HAVE A LIST OF QUANTIFIABLE GOALS?
Many parts of an appraisee's performance are measurable in
numeric terms. Make sure that any specific figures about what
is expected are made clear. These could be to cut costs by 10
percent on all budgets, or to prioritize finding at least two new
clients by a specific date. Very often, these goals are derived
from broader departmental goals that managers are given
by their supervisors.

How to set goals and objectives continued

5 WHAT DO I CONSIDER TO BE SUCCESSFUL PERFORMANCE?
Think about how you are going to measure success. Where goals are quantifiable, results will be clear, but it will be more difficult to assess something like "customer services." This is the bottom line because you will have to rate each part of the appraisee's performance when next year's performance review meeting comes around.

6 WHAT ARE THE APPRAISEE'S DEVELOPMENT NEEDS?
Although creating a development plan requires considerable input from the appraisee, all managers will have an opinion on whether effort is being concentrated in the right areas, and whether it will be successful.

7 HOW WILL I PROPOSE THESE GOALS AND OBJECTIVES?
Remember that you are the manager and that you are
answerable for what the appraisee does. This means that
you may have to be tough-minded when it comes to setting
goals. Also bear in mind that the purpose of the performance
review is to gain understanding of what needs to be done.
Agreement is not the aim.

8 IS IT APPROPRIATE FOR THE APPRAISEE TO FORMULATE GOALS, TOO?
This can be a useful way of motivating an employee to achieve
his own aims. Often, appraisee-led goals are a useful
supplement to those given by management.

The appraisee's perspective

Although as an appraisee, you will have little control over what goals and objectives you will be expected to meet over the coming year—these will largely be handed down by the manager, who will derive them from broader departmental goals set by his own supervisor—there are still several points to consider. It always pays to be prepared for the meeting. Several of these points mirror those that the manager must consider.

1 DO YOU HAVE A CLEAR IDEA OF YOUR ORGANIZATION'S MISSION STATEMENT, VALUES, AND VISION?
You can expect to have goals and objectives set for you that further the broader vision of your company.

2 WHAT ARE YOUR MAIN TASKS AND RESPONSIBILITIES?
Look at your job description to find out exactly what you are supposed to be doing. Also be ready to articulate how your job has changed or transformed since your last review.

3 WHAT DO YOU THINK YOUR GOALS SHOULD BE?
Assess your own performance over the past year and see what you would like to accomplish over the coming year. Do this with reference to the two preceding points.

4 DO YOU KNOW WHAT COMPETENCIES YOU ARE EXPECTED
TO DEMONSTRATE?
Arrange a quick meeting with your manager to find out what
your core competencies are (the behaviors all employees must
demonstrate) and the job-based competencies (the ones you
are expected to demonstrate for your particular role).

5 ARE YOU READY TO DISCUSS THESE POINTS WITH YOUR APPRAISER?
Be prepared to talk confidently about your role and how you
would like to grow in your job.

PERSONAL DEVELOPMENT PLANS

There is one area where you have
great input into what happens.
This is the personal development
plan. These plans document
activities that are designed to
continuously improve an individual's
skills. They include ideas for working
more effectively and taking on more
responsibilities. Your manager will
need to determine whether he
thinks that these are effective before
allowing you to implement them.
We will look further at what these
plans might contain on pp. 204–207.

It is also important that you
write your personal development
plan down, and make it a part of
your appraisal. Its effectiveness
and success will have to be
assessed, like all the other parts of
your job, at next year's
performance review meeting.

Setting goals for results and behaviors

It is important to distinguish between two different issues. One is "what" the results are. The other is "how" the results are achieved.

1

The "What" part of the equation is the results achieved.

These are examples of results:

- Outputs
- Products manufactured
- Percentage increases
- Financial data
- Budgets
- Customer returns
- Quantities produced
- Deadlines
- Projects completed
- Time saved

2

The "How" part of the equation is the behaviors demonstrated in achieving those results.

These are examples of behaviors:

- Regard for organizational values and vision
- Regard for core and job-based competencies
- Attitude toward work
- Approach to problems
- Job habits
- Work traits
- Collaborative spirit
- Leadership

Ultimately, companies are more interested in results than how they are achieved because results translate into revenue. But this does not mean that behaviors can be ignored. For example, consider the advertising executive who produces great commercials that clients love and that sell products, but he uses copyrighted material without permission and bullies models and photographers on the photoshoots so that no one will work with him again. Clearly the results are right (client satisfaction), but the behaviors are wrong. In fact, he will get the company a bad name, which will eventually damage the business. Conversely, an employee who shares the corporate vision of producing goods to the highest standards but neglects to pay attention to budgets, with the result that profitability falls dramatically, is also going to damage a company. A balance must be found between results and behaviors.

Key job responsibilities

Realizing what the key job responsibilities of the appraisee are is part of the goal-setting process. How else can you make sure that the appraisee is concentrating his efforts on the right areas? Allied to this is working out which responsibilities carry the most weight.

Make a list of your appraisee's responsibilities. This should be brief. There is no need to go over every detail of the dozens of actual tasks each employee has to juggle every day. This is an assessment to see where the major areas of contribution are. Every job can be broken down into its component responsibilities, from the new administrative assistant to the CEO. Take the example of a publishing director.

HE WILL HAVE THE FOLLOWING RESPONSIBILITIES:

1 Present ideas

2 Commission authors

3 Negotiate contracts

4 Manage budgets

5 Represent the company

These then are the areas that goals and objectives should be set in.

WHICH IS THE MOST IMPORTANT?
There are two ways in which to determine which parts of the job are most important. First, look at the bottom line. Which of these responsibilities will most contribute to the long-term profitability of the job? Arguably negotiating the contract is most important. A badly negotiated contract can lose a company a lot of money by placing expensive burdens on it.

Another way is to ask the appraisee to decide which is the one key area of his job that you would have him do above any other and that you consistently require and depend upon him to complete successfully.

What goals should I set?

Goals can relate to any of the key areas of individual, departmental, or organizational activities, and usually a combination of all three.

SOME OF THE "HANDS-ON" PLACES TO THINK ABOUT WHEN SETTING GOALS:

1

THE COMPANY MISSION STATEMENT,
OR THE COMPANY'S VALUES AND VISIONS
This is a good place to start looking—working toward the broader goals of your company is essential. It means that the mission statement stuck to your noticeboard is not just another piece of management jargon.

2

MANAGEMENT GOALS
Passing the goals that your own supervisor, and his supervisor in turn, set along the line to your subordinates ensures that managerial aims are consistent. Managerial goals are likely to be departmental in scope, and breaking down the objectives set by management into goals that all the individuals that make up the department can achieve is an important task.

3 KEY JOB RESPONSIBILITIES
We looked at key job responsibilities in the previous section.
What goals would encourage the employee to improve his
main areas of responsibility?

4 INCOMPLETE OR UNFULFILLED GOALS FROM THE LAST APPRAISAL
Where these are still relevant (and longer-term goals may
also be relevant), reset the goal for the coming period. Discuss
with the appraisee whether he has gathered the skills and
experience during the past year that will enable him to reach
the goal this year.

5 CUSTOMERS AND CLIENTS
Think about how well a service or product is provided to a
customer or client. For these purposes, a "customer" can be
another department or colleague, as well as external clients who
are paying for a particular service. Ask them (where appropriate)
where their greatest needs are, and use these as a building block
for developing goals that would best serve those needs.

Setting effective goals

Identifying the right goals in the right areas are the first steps in setting goals and objectives. But how do you provide a brief to achieve this? A helpful way of making this decision is to look at the "SMART" acronym.

SMART

SPECIFIC   MEASURABLE   ATTAINABLE   RELEVANT   TIME BOUND

SPECIFIC

Provide specific details of the objective, leaving no room for indecision or error. Asking the appraisee to "write better reports" is poor. A much better goal would be to "write reports following an agreed-upon structure, with a 100-word introduction, 200 words of main findings, followed by a 10-point summary, finishing with a 50-word conclusion. Make sure all facts are double-checked."

MEASURABLE

The goal should have some evidence of successful completion. This means that the goal should be measurable or quantifiable in terms of efficiency and effectiveness.

ATTAINABLE

The goal must be within the appraisee's abilities and control. Asking an appraisee to open two new client accounts by the end of the month, when this is typically a year's work is not an attainable objective. Nothing is more demotivating for an employee than being set up to fail. This does not mean, however, that goals should be easily attainable. Challenging, high standards that are still realistic are discussed in the next section (see pp. 220–223).

Ideally, your objectives should also reflect an agreement between the appraisee and the manager. However, agreement does not mean that unless the appraisee agrees to the goal it cannot be set. It means that the two parties agree that the objective is valid—in short, that the appraisee understands what is being set and why.

RELEVANT
Setting goals that are relevant neither to departmental aims nor to the wider aims of the organization are a mismanagement of resources. You must bear in the mind the larger picture when setting individual goals—how will they benefit the department (or team) and, ultimately, company?

TIMEBOUND
A clear timeframe for completion of the goals must be provided. For example, "reports must be completed and e-mailed to me by 5 P.M. each Friday," or that "a new client account will be opened six months from the date of this meeting."

Setting standards

So what standards can you realistically expect your appraisee to meet? Do you analyze the capabilities, intelligence, or skills and experience of each appraisee and set standards accordingly, setting more demanding goals for more capable employees and easier ones for less capable ones? Or do you ignore individual employee capabilities and adopt a one-size-fits-all approach to standards? Or do you set standards in accordance with the demands and expectations of the job?

Remember that the whole performance review system is based on objectivity. You must ask yourself, "What needs to be done, and how will it be carried out?" This means that the level you set your standards to is decided by the current demands of the job. This automatically answers the "what needs to be done" part of the issue.

"How will it be carried out" must be discussed with the appraisee, with regard to the size and length of the task, the current structure and resources of your department, and the individual development plans for the appraisee (which must provide a motivational challenge). "How it will be carried out" is variable, therefore. What doesn't change is "what needs to be done." You cannot excuse someone from doing their job—you're not a teacher forgiving a student for not doing his homework.

BEING STRONG-MINDED
This means that in some circumstances you will be breaking bad news to your appraisee by setting goals that have standards that he may regard as too high. You must stand your ground. Tread carefully

though when explaining what needs to be done, and make sure you have the reasons behind the goals at your fingertips. Say something like: "We must increase our sales by 10 percent this year. I know that this sounds a lot in the prevailing market conditions, but our competitors are seeing year-on-year increases in this field, and we have a lot of catching up to do. Our departmental figures were poor last year and must be turned around." No one can argue with your logic—you are losing sales and will eventually go out of business. Gaining acceptance and understanding from your team members in this way is important in setting reasonable objectives.

If the appraisee says, "But I'm already working a 12-hour day and traveling on weekends. What you're asking is impossible," your answer to this is to discuss, with the active input from the appraisee, how resources (time, finances, and staff) can be redeployed or reorganized so that these tough standards can become realistically achievable. You then explain how exciting and satisfying a challenge this presents, and how it ties into his development plan.

Communicating goals

Identifying what the goals are is the first and most important step. Communicating them is the next task. Without exception, write them down. Otherwise, either no one will remember what was said in six months' time, or they will have misinterpreted your instructions.

Ideally, your goals should be briefly listed, be direct, and, as always, be specific. List one goal at a time, and do not add in any extraneous detail. Clarity and precision are the aims here. It is also a good idea to add weight to your goal list. Make this clear to the appraisee, and set up some way of showing this, for example, by listing your goals in order of priority.

YOUR GOALS SHOULD BE CONSTRUCTED AS FOLLOWS:

1

USE IMPERATIVE VERBS
These include "increase," "expand," "create," "reduce," "control," "write," and "design." They convey a specific, single action.

2

ADD IN TIMESCALES AND BUDGETS
Designing a passenger lounge is likely to be expensive and take months. So say: "Design a passenger lounge for business-class passengers that interfaces with portable office equipment. Total design cost not to exceed $1 million and final plans to be completed by end of October this year."

3 STATE THE DESIRED RESULT
Attach a quantity or other method of measurement to this.
This could be something like "Reduce mail order returns by
10 percent," or "Design a passenger lounge for business-class
passengers that interfaces with portable office equipment."
There is no quantifiable measurement in the passenger lounge
example, so say that the success criteria are the number of
favorable comments on focus-group satisfaction reviews.

4 ADD IN TIMES FOR REVIEWS AND FEEDBACK
This makes the final goal: "Design a passenger lounge
for business-class passengers that interfaces with portable
office equipment. Total design cost not to exceed $1 million
and final plans to be completed by end of October this year.
First review meeting to be held end of May. Next review
meeting to be held end of August."

Repeat this process for each of the goals to complete your goal list.

Discussing development

Development activities are devised to help appraisees achieve both short- and long-term objectives. It is clearly in the interests of all managers to have their staff continuously improve their capabilities. This will be of obvious benefit to their department and the organization as a whole. Because development is concerned with short- and long-term goals, be sure to find out what the appraisee's career aspirations are, and how development can point him in the right direction, as well as addressing the current day-to-day issues.

PERSONAL DEVELOPMENT PLANS
Typically, these activities are fully documented on a Personal Development Plan (PDP), which forms part of the appraisal paperwork.

THE PDP SETS OUT:

1

DEVELOPMENT NEEDS
It is up to the appraisee to identify his development needs, although these need to be agreed on by the manager, who may also have strong feelings about certain areas that need specific attention. Appraisees often need direction on how to identify developmental needs and resources, so make sure you are prepared to discuss these. Developmental needs should be brief and address specific areas for improvement. For example, if time management is the issue, development needs could be "To learn how to prioritize tasks, delegate, and meet deadlines."

2 ACTIVITIES THAT WILL ADDRESS THOSE NEEDS
Activities can be on-the-job experience and training, or an
external training course or seminar. Find out what method
of learning the appraisee gets the best results from. This
information will provide the best development activity.
Also think about what tasks a manager can set an employee
to stretch him. Challenges are a great way to create
opportunities for development.

3 WHEN
Set a clear timeframe with the appraisee for when any
development activity will take place.

4 RESULTS
What did the appraisee actually learn? What impact has this
had on the appraisee's performance at work, with particular
reference to areas for improvement?

Discussing development continued

5 MANAGER'S ASSESSMENT
Fill in here whether or not the plan for this particular
development need produced expected results or not. If results
are not easily quantifiable (and in many instances they will not
be), then managers must think in advance about what the
criteria they will use to judge success are. To evaluate
development, consider:

- Planning regular review meetings
- If, and how, appraisees have applied their new skills to
  their work
- Assess improvements to performance
- Record results in writing on the PDP

THESE ARE SOME DEVELOPMENT ACTIVITIES:

ON-THE-JOB:

- Shadowing a co-worker
- Temporary transferal to
  another department
- Mentoring
- Assuming agreed-on, monitored,
  extra responsibilities

EXTERNAL TRAINING:

- Attending courses
- Participating in workshops
- Attending conferences
- Studying for further
  professional qualifications

REVIEWING DEVELOPMENT NEEDS

No business environment remains the same for long, and this is particularly true in today's marketplace. This means that development needs will change as individual and departmental needs change. As a manager, it is up to you to monitor these changes, and in the context of performance review, consider whether the appraisee's developmental needs are changing as well. To this end, arrange regular meetings to assess and review the relevance of the PDP.

This particularly applies if the appraisee's role is changing, either because of business changes or because of promotion or departmental restructuring. You will have to identify—with the active input of the appraisee—where new development needs are and check that appropriate resources are available to meet these new needs. Also be aware that the criteria by which you judge the success or otherwise of any development activity may also have to change to reflect the changing circumstances.

Thinking about training

Training courses are expensive and time-consuming and keep your employee away from his desk. This means that you must choose carefully when agreeing to send an employee on one.

However, typically training does play a valuable part in nearly all PDPs if used wisely, so you will have to decide what part it should play and where it fits in.

THESE ARE THE POINTS YOU SHOULD CONSIDER:

1

DETERMINE WHAT AREAS NEED IMPROVEMENT
Identify the problem areas where employee performance is poor, and think about how this area might be best improved. Many areas can be improved by on-the-job training or experience, but where a specific set of key pieces of knowledge is needed, then consider a training course.

2

MAKE SURE THAT THE EMPLOYEE WILL ACTUALLY LEARN SOMETHING RELEVANT
This sounds obvious, but the employee must learn a new skill or piece of knowledge that has a direct impact on his ability to do his job. Training should not be used just to create a well-rounded employee.

3 DECIDE HOW TO PUT THE NEW SKILLS OR KNOWLEDGE
TO IMMEDIATE USE
Make sure that the employee has a task to do that right away
makes use of his new abilities. This means that you must
also make sure that the timing of the course is right. If the
employee will not start on a project that requires new skills till
May, don't send him on a training course in February.

4 DETERMINE WHAT THE ORGANIZATION WILL GAIN BY SENDING AN
EMPLOYEE ON A TRAINING COURSE
Ultimately, your aim is to improve the bottom line for the
company. You need to consider whether the company's revenue
will increase as a result of training.

Action plans

After all the objectives, goals, and development needs have been discussed (and preferably agreed on), the appraisee will need to produce an action plan.

The action plan breaks down into bite-size chunks of what is to be done, who is responsible for what parts of the job, and when each part needs to be completed, distilled from the goal list and PDP.

It is mainly the appraisee's job to produce the action plan—he is the one who will have to commit to it, so he should be the one to write it.

Ideally, your company will have a standard form to fill out, but a planning diary will do just as well.

You need to be involved in the action plan, as you may be involved in certain tasks, such as alerting people to the fact the appraisee has new authority to act in certain situations or implementing some of the development activities.

A GOOD ACTION PLAN FOLLOWS MANY OF THE SAME RULES AS COMMUNICATING GOALS (SEE PP. 202–203). IT SHOULD:

1 Be brief, concise, and specific.

2 Use imperative verbs; literally, a call to action.

3 State the desired result; for example, "Gain authorization."

4 State the subject matter clearly; for example, "Gain authorization to attend policy overview meetings."

5 State who is involved; for example, "Gain authorization to attend policy overview meetings from the head of marketing and the HR director."

6 State initials of those involved in carrying out the action. Make sure that someone is accountable for each of the actions, including yourself.

7 State the date by which the action must be completed.

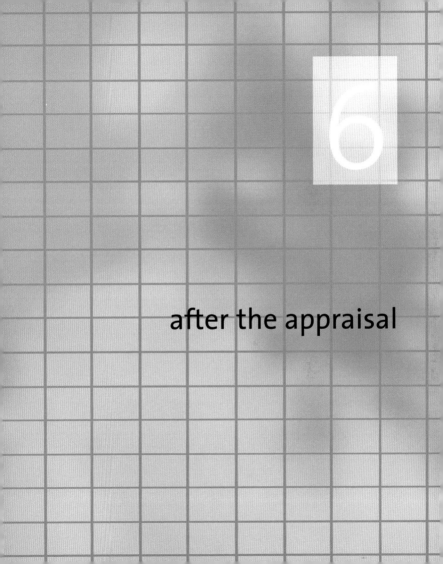

6

after the appraisal

after the appraisal

The follow-up for the manager

For a manager, the follow-up is as crucial as the preparation for the appraisal meeting and the meeting itself.

THE MANAGER MUST:

1 MOTIVATE EMPLOYEES BY CREATING AND PERPETUATING THE CONDITIONS THAT MOTIVATE
Employees will be better able to reach their objectives if their manager is able to create an environment in which they can excel.

2 CORRECT ANY PERFORMANCE PROBLEMS
As the year progresses, assess how performance is progressing, and take the necessary steps to correct any problems.

3 REVIEW GOALS AND OBJECTIVES
Typically, some goals will change over the course of the year, as projects evolve and business needs change. The manager needs to keep the employee's performance and developmental goals aligned with these changes.

4 ADHERE TO THEIR ROLE IN THE DEVELOPMENT PLAN
The manager will have some part to play in the PDP. She must
bear her tasks and responsibilities in mind as the year progresses.

5 GIVE FEEDBACK ON EMPLOYEE'S WORK PERFORMANCE
Feedback is not just a once a year exercise. The manager needs
to conduct regular meetings to give feedback on the
employee's performance. Bear in mind that it is also the
appraisee's responsibility to ask for feedback as well.

6 KEEP TRACK OF PERFORMANCE
The only way to keep abreast of what the employee is doing is
to write down achievements and areas for improvement. This is
best done in a performance diary, which provides essential
information for completing next year's appraisal form.

The follow-up for the appraisee

AS AN APPRAISEE, YOU HAVE FOLLOW-UP RESPONSIBILITIES, TOO. YOU MUST:

1
MEET THE GOALS AND OBJECTIVES AGREED IN THE PERFORMANCE
REVIEW MEETING
Clearly, doing the job and meeting the prescribed goals
are the backbone of the employee's responsibilities in
the follow-up phase.

2
ALERT THE MANAGER TO CHANGES IN OBJECTIVES
Ultimately, no one knows their job as well as the person who is
actually doing it. So while the manager needs to keep abreast
of changing goals, the person best placed to realize that project
demands are changing is the appraisee herself.

3
ALERT THE MANAGER TO NEED FOR FEEDBACK
Managers have to juggle several different tasks and are often
pressed for time. This means that arranging meetings to
provide the employee with constructive feedback is easily
sacrificed in favor of more pressing day-to-day issues.
Gently remind the manager that a short meeting to provide
feedback is essential to your development.

4 ADHERE TO THE DEVELOPMENT PLAN, AND ALERT THE MANAGER TO HER ROLE IN THE PLAN
Having written the PDP, the appraisee must carry it out. Bear in mind that the manager may have to be reminded to do her agreed-on tasks to facilitate any relevant parts of the plan.

5 WRITE DOWN ACCOMPLISHMENTS (AND NOTE FAILURES, TOO)
List your achievements (and failures) so you have a comprehensive list to refer to when asked to complete the self-assessment before the next appraisal meeting. Keep these notes in a journal, with weekly or bi-weekly notations.

Contributing fully in the follow-up shows a commitment to the appraisal system as a whole. An appraisal system in which everyone acknowledges their roles and responsibilities ultimately helps everybody in the organization.

after the appraisal

Review meetings

As we have mentioned, checking progress is not just a once-a-year obligation on the manager's part. The employee's performance needs to be reviewed regularly. These reviews are best carried out in meetings (different types of review meeting are described here) to make sure milestones are being met on their way to achieving their goals and objectives.

As the manager, you need to have a clear idea of what should have been achieved at each review meeting, which is a good reason to keep your performance diary up-to-date.

USE A DIFFERENT TYPE OF MEETING FOR DIFFERENT SITUATIONS:

1 CATCH-UP
Use this type of meeting to discuss informally a specific topic, or simply as a quick update. This is useful when something important has just happened that is going to have an impact on the employee, the team, or a particular objective.

2 MILESTONE REVIEW
This is a more formal meeting, arranged in advance with an agenda, to discuss whether particular milestones have been reached on the journey to achieving an objective. This meeting ensures that everything is going to plan.

3 FULL REVIEW

A formally arranged meeting at the end of important projects or pieces of work. These ensure that goals and objectives have been met, and that they were relevant when set. Use this meeting as a valuable overview session to establish what has been achieved and what has been learned.

Choose a review meeting that is appropriate for the appraisee, what she is doing, and her level of experience. For example, an established team member doing a job she is experienced in will require far fewer milestone meetings than a new employee with a difficult project, who would clearly benefit from lots of quick catch-ups.

Beware of scheduling meetings only when a problem arises. The purpose of a review meeting is to establish progress and assess whether objectives are being met.

Motivating employees

The nuts and bolts of any job are done by the members of the team or department you manage. Part of any manager's goal is to motivate employees to do their jobs to the best of their abilities by creating an environment in which this can happen.

1 **CHANCES FOR REAL ACCOMPLISHMENTS AND ACHIEVEMENT**
Setting goals and objectives is crucial to providing the opportunity to really accomplish something. The goals should stretch the employee, as well as allow him to take on more responsibility and do different tasks. This makes the job worth doing and avoids the feeling of just doing the 9 to 5 grind, where nothing changes.

2 **RECOGNITION OF EMPLOYEE ACCOMPLISHMENT**
Once the employee has accomplished something new, she will need it recognized. Official recognition is a valuable way of demonstrating to the employee that her work is valued by the company. See pp. 224–225 for more on recognition.

3 **MONEY AND CAREER ADVANCEMENT**
A large monthly paycheck and the promise of corporate advancement are obvious powerful motivators for many career-minded people.

4 **SETTING A PERSONAL CHALLENGE**
Constant repetition of the same task, or set of tasks, becomes boring. Providing a challenge—a new, achievable task that requires effort, initiative, and commitment—is a valuable way to ensure that employees use their skills and intelligence positively.

5 **PERSONAL SATISFACTION FROM WORK AND ACCOMPLISHMENTS**
It always feels great to sit back and think: "Yes, I managed to do that. It was really hard, and at times I doubted whether I could succeed, but in the end, I saw it through." This has nothing to do with whether the boss is happy with the work or not. It is a personal feeling that will have positive repercussions in all areas of an employee's life, not just work.

6 **CHANCE TO ACT WITH SOME DISCRETION AND AUTONOMY**
An environment where the employee is allowed a degree of freedom (the degree is to be decided by the manager) is a good idea. Having a supervisor looking over an employee's shoulder, constantly telling her what to do at every turn, quickly makes the employee dependent on the supervisor's input for every decision, and her own input worthless.

Motivating employees continued

7

OTHER MOTIVATORS
These can include many small but significant factors, such as additional vacation time, an upgrade in title, the latitude to hire an assistant, better office space, permission to attend professional conferences, and professional opportunities that are not a part of the developmental part of the appraisal.

NEGATIVE FACTORS
Concentrating your efforts in boosting these areas of an employee's work will be highly motivational. But at the same time, the following negative factors need to be reduced; otherwise, they will take the shine off the positive ones.

1

POOR PAY AND POOR BENEFITS
Receiving low pay does not encourage great performance. However, you may not be in a position to increase an employee's pay radically. Emphasize that good performance means a good appraisal rating, which will lead to a pay raise, and promotional opportunities. You can radically increase job satisfaction by genuinely saying "Thank you" for a job well done, and offering more pleasant tasks to do than the one just completed. See pp. 224–225 for more on recognition.

2 POOR WORKING CONDITIONS

These are easier to address. Is your employee's office dirty, too hot, too cold, or cluttered with old files? A spring clean is a great way to create the feeling of a fresh start, breaking free from past projects and getting focused and organized. In addition, air conditioning units/heaters are inexpensive and can provide welcome ventilation.

3 POOR ATTITUDES FROM WORKERS

Negativity from workers about the "impossible" goals and objectives being set by management "upstairs" can be very disruptive and will result in a "can't-do" attitude from co-workers. Find out why there is problem, try to address it, and explain what the employees' attitude is doing to team morale. You will also have to take a deep breath and tell the employees involved to end the disruption.

4 NANNYING COMPANY POLICY

Company policy that dictates how each moment of each day should be passed assumes everyone is a naughty child. Keep the number of rules about behavior to a minimum, and link them directly to job performance. Anything that does not affect performance or have a direct impact on the reputation of the company is not your affair.

Providing recognition

How and when to provide recognition can be difficult to gauge. As we have seen, recognizing achievement is a central tenet of motivating staff, so you will have to decide when and how to use it for the best effect.

WHAT IS RECOGNITION?

Recognition is acknowledgment of a job well done. It acts as a stamp of approval that we achieved a required result and acted in an acceptable way to get that result. We seek recognition for our achievements from parents, friends, and partners, and, in this instance, at work from bosses. Once we get it, we feel as if we have attained some kind of official standard.

Managers (and all those listed above) realize the power of recognition because it reinforces the idea that our behavior (and the results it brings) was correct. Thus, in turn, we are more likely to behave that way again in the future, so bringing about repeated success. It also has the happy side-effect of making the recipient of recognition feel valued and wanted.

WHEN TO USE IT

This is not as obvious as it seems. Recognition needs to given only where it is merited. This begs the question, what should be considered "merit?" This links back to the section on setting standards—which should be high (see pp. 200–201). Merit should be given at work when someone has stretched themselves to a level they had not previously reached, or when they have achieved a challenging set of goals and objectives set in the performance review meeting.

This means that you should use it sparingly and with care. If you use it every time someone completes a simple task correctly, it quickly loses its motivational power. This also means that it should be used sparingly when a well-established employee completes a complex task, but one she has done many times. Only if the employee has outperformed himself should you recognize her performance. Conversely, it is much more appropriate to recognize good performance in a newcomer beginning a challenging project.

Finally, too much praise can be patronizing and can make people feel like well-behaved dogs about to be rewarded with a biscuit.

SO WHEN YOU ARE RECOGNIZING GOOD PERFORMANCE:

- Say specifically what the recognition is for.

- Say specifically what was good about the performance.

- Say specifically why the performance is being recognized in terms of how it fits into the bigger picture of departmental or organizational goals.

- Say if the recognition carries any specific reward (for example, a more desirable project to work on next time).

- Say a genuine "Thank you."

Dealing with poor performance

Despite all your best efforts to motivate your employees to achieve their goals and objectives and fulfill their development plan, some will not respond, and you will have to deal with poor performance.

BEFORE YOU DO ANYTHING, MAKE SURE THAT YOU HAVE:

■ Made it clear what the employee is expected to achieve. Although overall goals should be clear from the objective-setting part of the performance review system, does the employee know what the component parts of achieving the goal are, and the standard each part needs to reach?

■ Made sure that the employee can do the job. This means that you will have to check that she has the skills and experience she needs. For example, check that any key points on her development plan have been executed, or that a particular training course has been attended before you give someone a job they might not yet be able to do.

■ Informally told the employee that her performance is not up to standard. Suddenly launching into a discussion about poor performance will understandably upset an employee if this is the first she has heard about it. Have a quiet word to start with—if things don't improve, take the more formal line.

■ Fulfilled your part of the bargain. Have you done the things you said you would do in the development plan to facilitate success? These include informing other staff and departments about any new activities the employee might be taking on so the path is smoothed and obstacles removed.

WHAT TO SAY

If these issues have not been addressed, then you must do so first. You, as the manager, have your part to play in your employees' success. Once you have got your own house in order and employee performance still does not improve, then you must take steps to correct it. Usually a formal meeting is a good idea. Make sure you know what you are going to say before you start the meeting. This involves:

■ Stating that there is a performance problem that you must address.

■ Stating exactly what the problem is. This means clarifying what you want the employee to do as compared to what the employee is actually doing. You must have clear evidence to back up any assertions made.

■ Using active listening to find out what the employee has to say for herself. There may be a reason for the poor performance that you are not aware of. You can then address the problem.

Dealing with poor performance continued

- Explaining what the consequences are for the team or department of the poor performance. Do not make it personal by saying: "Your poor performance is going to have dire consequences if you don't pull your socks up." Such threats tend to produce defensive reactions.

- Gently getting the employee to agree that she is not doing what she is being paid to do, and gain a resolve from the employee to solve the problem.

IF THINGS DO NOT IMPROVE
When all of these points do not have any effect on performance, there is a need for disciplinary action. You must follow company procedure at all times, as advised by your own supervisor, HR, and, where necessary, your company's legal team. Disciplinary action will possibly spur your appraisee to legal action, so it is critical that every step you take is legally defensible. Regardless of what your company policy is, these are some points to bear in mind:

- Punishing employees rarely rectifies the problem. Often, it makes it less likely that the problem will be rectified.

- Ensuring the employee takes responsibility for her own actions, and the consequences of her actions, is essential.

Be clear about what the performance faults you need to rectify are, and what effect on your department and organization these faults are having. Always focus on performance problems. Do not let the issue become personal.

■ Suspending the employee is a last-step solution, though a very effective one. This makes it clear that the issue of poor performance is a serious one. Make it clear that commitment to the job is needed, or termination will follow. Some forward-thinking companies, especially those employing white-collar professionals, continue to pay employees during suspension. This removes the punishment aspect of suspension.

■ Always put every step in writing. It is essential that a proper paper trail exists. It must show that you made it clear to the employee that her performance was unacceptable, and that you gave her every chance to improve, or be asked to leave. Set a reasonable timeframe for every improvement you request and include this in the letter or memo you send.

■ Forward copies of every piece of correspondance to your HR department to be included in your employee's file.

Dealing with teams

Performance reviews focus on assessing the performance and development of individuals. However, it can be useful to include the whole team in parts of the performance review system, particularly with regard to setting team objectives and motivation. Overall, this encourages teamwork, an essential part of a manager's goal.

However, bear in mind that appraising a team can be notoriously difficult to do and best avoided. Each individual will perform differently in different areas. Some will work harder than others; some will display different competencies and behaviors than others; some will be more results-oriented than others and so on. This means that attempting to appraise a team as you would an individual and apply a single rating is generally misleading and generally unfair to those who have worked the hardest.

Despite this, setting team objectives and sitting down with all the members of the team to discuss how these objectives may be best achieved is a worthwhile task because it:

1 Focuses efforts on objectives that need to be accomplished as a unit. Individual goals are ultimately the main focus of any appraisal, but it is useful for the team as a whole to understand how all these individual goals will be pulled together into common objectives.

2 Encourages team members to be open with each other, by giving constructive feedback to each other and to the manager. Peer-to-peer feedback is considered to be a very useful way of gaining a true picture of performance.

3 Helps clarify job-based competencies on a team-wide basis. For a team to function effectively, all members not only need to be completing their tasks successfully, they also need to be demonstrating common behaviors. These are principally how well the team runs meetings, communicates with each other, takes on board new ideas, and arrives at accurate conclusions.

Dealing with teams continued

4
Encourages members to share information and knowledge that may dovetail with individual development plans. Some team members will have more experience, skills, and knowledge than others. A team meeting can help clarify who can help whom with which areas of development.

5
Clarifies where training needs are, especially if several members of the team need the same training needs. Group training may be cheaper and easier to manage than having individuals attending courses separately.

6
Makes clear to the whole team how their collective efforts fit into the wider vision of the organization. This is important because it is much easier for a team to work together if they know the direction they are supposed to be heading in.

Arrange a meeting where all team members attend. Stress the importance of attendance and do not hold the meeting if anyone cannot attend, for whatever reason. This meeting must be all-inclusive. Set an agenda and distribute it to every team member in advance.

What team objectives do you want to talk about?

Then you need to explain how individual objectives fit into the larger picture of team ones. This will ensure that everyone understands the overall goal and is pulling the same direction.

1 Get everyone to write down what part each of them plays in meeting team objectives. Make sure that everyone's tasks are clear and that they understand the action they need to take to complete their tasks successfully.

2 Explain what the roles of the team members in the meeting are.

3 Be prepared to listen actively and to take on board the suggestions of your team members. Some will have ideas that may be better than yours.

Thinking about management skills

Implementing a performance review system is not easy, and many managers dread the whole process, especially the review meeting. This means that there is always plenty of scope for improvement as regards manager's appraisal skills.

YOU CAN MEASURE YOUR OWN SUCCESS IN ADMINISTERING THE SYSTEM BY ASKING THE FOLLOWING QUESTIONS:

1 HAS YOUR SUBORDINATES' PERFORMANCE IMPROVED?
Ultimately, this is the million dollar question. All your assessments, feedback, and motivational efforts culminate in this one crucial area. You should start to see improvements filtering through after two or three months.

2 DO YOUR REVIEW MEETINGS (SEE PP. 218–219) SHOW THAT IMPROVEMENTS ARE BEING MADE?
This applies not only to those who were previously performing poorly but also to good performers seeking to improve further.

3 HAVE I CREATED AN ENVIRONMENT THAT MOTIVATES EMPLOYEES?
Analyze which factors you have not yet addressed or could address more effectively to create a better environment.

4 HOW EFFICIENTLY HAVE I FULFILLED MY END OF THE BARGAIN?
This means that you need to find out how effective you have
been in facilitating success and removing barriers to it. Were
you timely with your actions, or did you have to be reminded by
an indignant and frustrated employee?

5 WHAT ARE MY FACE-TO-FACE SKILLS LIKE?
Consider how well you came across when directly addressing
the appraisee, in all the situations where face-to-face contact
occurred. Think about how you used active listening and the
right body language, gave effective, constructive feedback, set
objectives, and handled performance problems by directly
addressing them.

Consider where your own weaknesses are in these areas and think about how
you might go about improving, as if you were the appraisee.

Index